W9-CCU-645

Microsoft®

Office 2003

New Features Guide

Changes from Office XP to Office 2003

THOMSON

COURSE TECHNOLOGY

Australia • Canada • Mexico • Singapore • Spain • United Kingdom • United States

Microsoft® Office 2003 **New Features Guide**   Changes from Office XP to Office 2003

VP and GM of Courseware:	Michael Springer
Series Product Managers:	Caryl Bahner-Guhin, Charles G. Blum, and Adam A. Wilcox
Developmental Editor:	Leslie Caico
Production Editor:	Patty Stephan
Series Designer:	Adam A. Wilcox
Cover Designer:	Nancy Goulet
Key Tester:	Bill Bateman

COPYRIGHT © 2004 Course Technology, a division of Thomson Learning, Inc. Thomson Learning™ is a trademark used herein under license.

For more information, contact Course Technology, 25 Thomson Place, Boston, Massachusetts, 02210.

Or find us on the World Wide Web at: www.course.com

ALL RIGHTS RESERVED. No part of this work covered by the copyright hereon may be reproduced or used in any form or by any means—graphic, electronic, or mechanical, including photocopying, recording, taping, Web distribution, or information storage and retrieval systems—without the written permission of the publisher.

For permission to use material from this text or product, contact us by
Tel (800) 730-2214
Fax(800) 730-2215
www.thomsonrights.com

Trademarks
Course Technology and the Course Technology logo are registered trademarks used under license. All other names and visual representations used herein are for identification purposes only and are trademarks and the property of their respective owners.

Microsoft Windows NT, Microsoft Windows 2000, and Microsoft Windows XP are either trademarks or registered trademarks of Microsoft Corporation in the United States and/or other countries. Microsoft is a registered trademark of Microsoft Corporation in the United States and/or other countries. Course Technology is an independent entity from the Microsoft Corporation and not affiliated with Microsoft in any manner.

Disclaimers
Course Technology reserves the right to revise this publication and make changes from time to time in its content without notice.

ISBN 0-619-25560-9

Printed in Canada

2 3 4 5 WC 06 05 04 03

Contents

Unit 1
Common features of Office 2003

Unit time: 60 minutes

Complete this unit, and you'll know how to:

A Use the Web-based Assistance feature to access online help.

B Download additional templates and clip art from the Web, use fax services, use Office Marketplace, and check for Office 2003 updates.

C Use Instant Messaging and the Research task pane.

Topic A: Getting help

Explanation

In Office 2003, Microsoft has introduced features that conveniently link applications to online content. You can search for information not only on your computer but also on the Web. The Help task pane provides an efficient way to find information online without opening the Internet Explorer window.

Assistance

Sometimes, you might need to search for information that is not available in the help provided within an Office application. In such cases, you can use the Assistance feature to search for information on the Web.

To use Assistance:

1   Start an Office application.

2   Choose Help, Microsoft Office Help to open the Help task pane for the application.

3   In the task pane, click the Assistance hyperlink to open the Microsoft Office Assistance Web page.

4   Under the BROWSE ASSISTANCE section, select the Office application for which you want help.

5   In the upper-right corner of the Web page, click the Search link.

6   In the Search for box, type the keyword or phrase you want to search for.

7   Click the "Click to search" button to display a list of links to Web pages that contain the specified keyword. Click any link to navigate to its corresponding Web page and view the page contents.

8   Close the browser window.

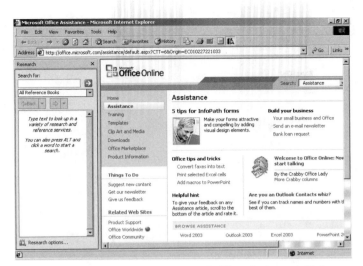

Exhibit 1-1: An example of the Microsoft Office Assistance Web page

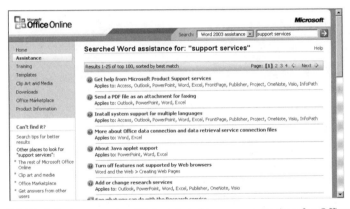

Exhibit 1-2: An example of links related to support services for Office 2003 products

Do it!

A-1: Using Assistance

Here's how	Here's why
1 Start Microsoft Office Word 2003	(Click Start, and choose Programs, Microsoft Office, Microsoft Office Word 2003.) A blank document appears.
2 Choose **Help**, **Microsoft Office Word Help**	To open the Word Help task pane.
3 In the Word Help task pane, under Microsoft Office Online, click **Assistance**	To open the Microsoft Office Assistance Web page. An example is shown in Exhibit 1-1, though the content and structure of this Web site is likely to change over time.
Maximize the window	If necessary.
4 Click	(The Research task pane button is on the Standard toolbar.) To close the Research task pane, if necessary.
5 Under BROWSE ASSISTANCE, click **Word 2003**	To open the Microsoft Office Word 2003 Assistance Web page.
In the second Search box, type **support services**	
	(This is in the upper-right part of the page.) You'll search for information on support services available for Microsoft Word 2003.
Click	(The Click to search button is to the right of the Search for box.) To display a list of links to Web pages that provide information on support services. An example of this list is shown in Exhibit 1-2.
6 Close the browser window	(Choose File, Close.) To return to Word.

Topic B: Web-related features

Explanation

Microsoft continually adds new templates, clip art, and utility software to its Web site. Office 2003 provides task panes that you can use to find and download such new components.

Downloading templates

Office applications, such as Word, Excel, and PowerPoint, provide built-in templates that you can use to create documents. However, these templates might not always meet your requirements. You can download additional templates from the Microsoft Office Online site. To do this:

1 Choose File, New to open the New Document task pane.

2 Click the Templates on Office Online link to open the Microsoft Office Templates Web page.

3 From the Microsoft Office Templates Web page, open a template for the current Office application.

4 Download the template. A new document will appear based upon it.

5 Close the browser window.

Exhibit 1-3: The New Document task pane

Do it!

B-1:   Using templates

Here's how	Here's why
1 Choose **File**, **New...**	The New Document task pane appears on the right side of the window, as shown Exhibit 1-3. You'll download a template to create a brochure.
2 In the New Document task pane, click as shown	Search online for: [ ] [Go] Templates on Office Online On my computer... To open the Microsoft Office Templates Web page.
3 Click as shown	Marketing Marketing Materials | Letters to Customers | Sales | More... To open the Microsoft Office Marketing Materials Web page.
4 Click **Brochures and Booklets**	Links to various brochure templates appear on the Web page.
5 Click **Brochure (Level theme)**	To open the Microsoft Office Brochure (Level theme) Web page. As with any Web page, the content and structure of this page might change over time.
6 Click **Download Now**	The template downloads, and then Word creates a new document based on it.
7 Observe the new document	It contains placeholder text in columns, sample graphics, and various styles you can use to create a professional-looking brochure.
8 Choose **File**, **Save As**	To open the Save As dialog box.
Navigate to the current unit folder	Within Student Data.
In the File name box, type **My brochure**	
Click **Save**	To save the document as a template.
9 Close the document	If a new Word window was opened during the process of opening the online template, close this window.
Close the browser window	

Downloading clip art

Explanation

Office 2003 provides a built-in clip art gallery that you can use to insert clip art in your documents. An online clip art gallery expands this selection, giving you even more options. You can download clip art from the online clip art gallery by using the Clip Art task pane.

To download clip art from the Web:

1　Choose Insert, Picture, Clip Art to open the Clip Art task pane.
2　Click the Clip art on Office Online link to open the Microsoft Office Clip Art and Media Web page.
3　Download the clip art you want to use.
4　Close the browser window.

To insert clip art:

1　In the Clip Art task pane, type a search criterion, and click Go.
2　In the document, place the insertion point where you want to insert the clip art.
3　Click the clip art to insert it.

Do it!

B-2:　Using clip art

Here's how	Here's why
1　Open Brochure	From the current unit folder. This document was created using a template downloaded from the Microsoft Web site.
Save the document as **My brochure**	(In the current unit folder.) A dialog box asks if you want to replace the existing file.
Click **OK**	
2　Choose **Insert**, **Picture**, **Clip Art...**	The Clip Art task pane appears on the right side of the window.
3　In the Clip Art task pane, click as shown	
	To open the Microsoft Office Clip Art and Media Web page. You'll download clip art from the Web.
4　Under BROWSE CLIP ART AND MEDIA, click **Food**	To open the Microsoft Office Food Web page.

5 Check as shown	 ☑ To add the item to the Selection Basket.
6 Observe the Selection Basket	**Selection Basket** Selected items: **1** Download size: **12 KB** (<1 min @ 56 Kbps) ――――――――― Review basket Download 1 item ⬇ (The Selection Basket is located on the left side of the screen.) The Selection Basket shows the items selected.
Click as shown	Download 1 item ⬇ (In the Selection Basket.) The Microsoft Office Download Web page appears.
7 Click **Download Now**	The File Download dialog box opens.
Select **Open this file from its current location**	
Click **OK**	To open the clip in the Microsoft Clip Organizer window.
Close the Clip Organizer window	
8 Close the browser window	
9 In the Clip Art task pane, in the Search for box, type **food**	
Click **Go**	The clip art you downloaded appears in the Clip Art task pane.

10 Click as shown

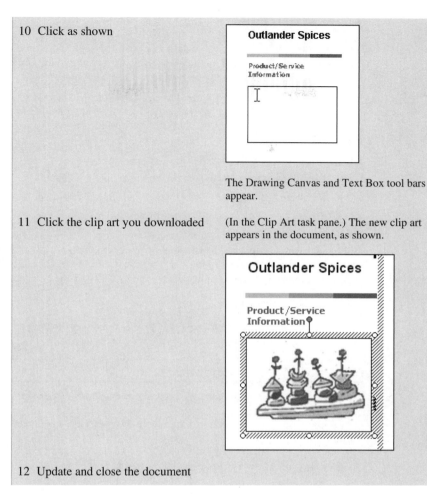

The Drawing Canvas and Text Box tool bars appear.

11 Click the clip art you downloaded

(In the Clip Art task pane.) The new clip art appears in the document, as shown.

12 Update and close the document

Faxing

Explanation Sending a fax is now as easy as sending an e-mail message. You can directly fax documents from Office 2003 applications by using one of two methods: You can either use a service provided by a service provider, or use a fax modem.

Fax services are supported by Word, Excel, PowerPoint, and Outlook, but you must have Word and Outlook installed to use these services, and Outlook must be open for you to send a fax. Together, Word and Outlook provide the necessary interface to send faxes.

The interface has the following fields:

- **Recipient name** — Used to specify the recipient's name
- **Fax number** — Used to specify the recipient's fax number
- **Subject** — Used to specify the subject of your fax

The fax document to be sent is automatically converted to a Tagged Image File Format (TIFF) image and is attached to an e-mail message. In the body of the e-mail message, you can type information about the fax. You can use the address book to fill in the fields. When specifying the country code, you need to start the code with a "+" symbol.

Advantages of fax services

The main advantage of using a fax service is that it reduces the time needed to send faxes. The following table lists some of the other advantages:

Advantage	Explanation
Mixed methods	You can fax a document to e-mail addresses and fax machines.
Multiple documents	You can attach multiple documents as a single package regardless of the number of pages in each document.
Electronic faxes	You can receive a fax in your Inbox as a TIFF attachment.
Offline scenario	You can compose a fax and store it in your Outbox. The fax is sent when the computer is connected to the network or is online.
Archives	You can store the sent faxes in the Outlook Sent Items folder or in another folder created in Outlook.

You can have more than one service provider for incoming faxes but only one service provider for outgoing faxes. If you want to use the fax service on more than one computer, your account needs to be registered on each computer; you do this by using a registration package from your fax service provider.

Do it!   **B-3: Using fax services to fax a Word document**

Here's how	Here's why
1 Create a blank document	You will fax this document.
2 Select **File**, **Send To**, **Recipient Using a Fax Modem...**	The Fax Wizard appears. You can use this wizard to specify the document to fax, the fax software, the recipients, the cover sheet, and sender information.
3 Click **Next**	The Which document do you want to send? screen appears. You can use this screen to select the document you want to send. You can also specify whether the fax will be sent with or without a cover sheet.
4 Click **Next**	The Which fax program do you want to use to send your fax? screen appears.
5 Select **A different fax program which is installed on this system**	To activate the listbox below.
Under Which of the following is your fax program?, select **MICROSOFT OFFICE DOCUMENT IMAGE**	In the list box.
6 Click **Next**	The Who should receive this fax? screen appears. You can either use the Address Book button to add addresses from your address book, or enter the addresses manually in the Name and Fax Number fields.
7 Click **Next**	The Which style do you want for your cover sheet? screen appears. You can select among Professional, Contemporary, or Elegant styles.
8 Click **Next**	The Who is the fax from? screen appears. Use this screen to specify the sender's information.
9 Click **Cancel**	
10 Close the document	

Office Marketplace

Explanation

You can download third-party software by using the Microsoft Office Marketplace. Third-party software can be used as add-in components with Microsoft Office applications.

To connect to Office Marketplace:

1 Choose Help, Microsoft Office Online to open the Microsoft Office Web page.
2 Under Home, click the Office Marketplace link to open the Microsoft Office Marketplace Web page.
3 Click the links for the services you want to use.
4 Close the browser window.

Exhibit 1-4: The DataPrompter 2003 add-in Web page

Do it!

B-4: Using Office Marketplace

Here's how	Here's why
1 Choose **Help,** **Microsoft Office Online**	To open the Microsoft Office Web page. You'll download an add-in that prompts you to enter data and then automatically inserts the data into a Microsoft Word document.
2 Under Home, click **Office Marketplace**	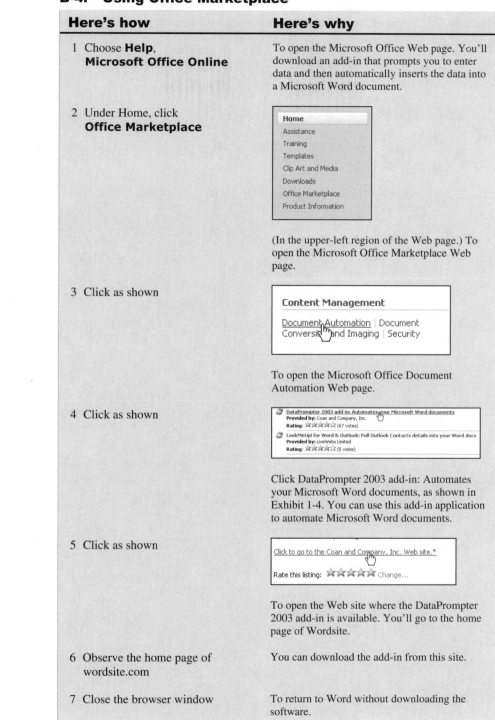 (In the upper-left region of the Web page.) To open the Microsoft Office Marketplace Web page.
3 Click as shown	To open the Microsoft Office Document Automation Web page.
4 Click as shown	Click DataPrompter 2003 add-in: Automates your Microsoft Word documents, as shown in Exhibit 1-4. You can use this add-in application to automate Microsoft Word documents.
5 Click as shown	To open the Web site where the DataPrompter 2003 add-in is available. You'll go to the home page of Wordsite.
6 Observe the home page of wordsite.com	You can download the add-in from this site.
7 Close the browser window	To return to Word without downloading the software.

Checking for Office updates

Explanation　Microsoft provides upgrade information and update patches on its Web site. You can keep track of new releases by using the Check for Updates feature that is available in all Office 2003 applications. For previous versions of Office, you had to go to the Microsoft Web site to check for updates; in Office 2003, however, you can access the same information from within an Office application.

To check for updates:

1　Choose Help, Check for Updates to open the Microsoft Office Downloads Web page in a browser window.

2　Click the Check for Updates link to check for available Office updates.

3　Close the browser window.

Do it!　## B-5: Searching the Web for updates

Here's how	Here's why
1　Choose **Help, Check for Updates**	(You might need to click the down chevron.) To open the Microsoft Office Downloads Web page.
2　Under Things To Do, click **Check for updates**	**Things To Do** Check for updates Suggest & Download Get our newsletter Give us feedback To open the Microsoft Office Update Web page. You use the Check for updates link to find Office 2003 applications that need to be updated.
3　Observe the Microsoft Office Update Web page	The Office applications that require updates will be listed on the Web page. You can update these applications by checking the required application name and clicking Start Installation.
4　Close the browser window	To return to Word without updating Office applications.

Topic C: Other features

Explanation Office 2003 includes several features you can use to communicate with other users and to search for information online. These features include Instant Messaging and the Research task pane. You can use Instant Messaging to communicate with your peers and clients located in any part of the world, as well as to keep track of your meetings and schedules. You can use the Research task pane to search for online information without switching between applications.

Instant Messaging

You can directly communicate with your online contacts by using the Instant Messaging feature. With Instant Messaging, you can send and receive messages instantaneously over the Internet or an intranet. This is unlike e-mail, for which you must send messages through and download messages from a server.

To send and receive instant messages, you can use *instant messengers*, which are stand-alone programs that you can download and install. An example of an instant messenger is MSN Messenger.

Instant Messaging in Office applications

Instant Messaging is available in various Office applications. Once this feature is set up, you can start an Instant Messaging conversation with someone by typing that person's e-mail address in your Office application. The Person Names smart tag appears near the person's name. Click the smart tag to open a shortcut menu, as shown in Exhibit 1-5. You can then choose the Send Instant Message option to send a message to your contact. Note that you can communicate only with a person who is online.

Exhibit 1-5: The Person Names smart tag

You can implement Instant Messaging in your Office applications by using any of the following technologies:

- **MSN Messenger Service** — Used to send instant messages to people on your contact list.
- **NetMeeting** — Used to participate in meetings over the Internet or an intranet.
- **Microsoft Windows SharePoint Services** — Used to share documents and information with people on a contact list.
- **Real-Time Communication (RTC) Server** — Used to create real-time communication functionality in your own application.

All these technologies use Microsoft Exchange Instant Messaging Service to run Instant Messaging.

Do it!

C-1:   Discussing Instant Messaging

Questions and answers

1 MSN Messenger is an instant messenger. True or false?

2 Which of the following technologies helps you share documents and information with people on a contact list?

A   Real-Time Communication (RTC) Server

B   Microsoft Windows SharePoint Services

C   NetMeeting

D   MSN Messenger Service

The Research task pane

Explanation

The Research service of Microsoft Office 2003 helps you seek information from online sources. This service is available in Office 2003 applications, except for Access and Outlook, through the Research task pane.

You can search for information online, on the Web, or on your computer. By using the Research task pane, you can easily insert definitions, stock quotes, and other research results into your documents. Using the Research task pane, you can also search multiple sources or select a specific source.

The following table lists the services provided by the Research task pane:

Item	Description
Dictionary	Search for words or phrases in the Microsoft Encarta English dictionary. You can also add other dictionaries, which are then compared against Encarta standards to ensure that you receive the best results. This occurs because Encarta does not provide all language-specific dictionaries, such as German, Korean, and Japanese.
Thesaurus	Search for synonyms and insert them into a document directly from the Research task pane. You can also click a result to look up additional words. You can look up words in the thesaurus of another language, such as French, Spanish, or Chinese.
Encyclopedia	Research your subject in Microsoft Encarta Encyclopedia. You can ask a question and review the results by using Encyclopedia.
Translation	Translate text by using bilingual dictionaries. You can translate single words or short phrases.
Stock quotes and company information	Seek stock quotes and company information while you work. If you aren't sure of a stock symbol or company name, then type a few words, and the search will find the symbol or name for you. You can also insert company information into a document and perform custom actions.
Intranet sites	Add your intranet site to the Research task pane for easy access.
Third-party services	Add third-party premium content to your list of research services, and Microsoft Office will present the most relevant information to you based on your search and question.

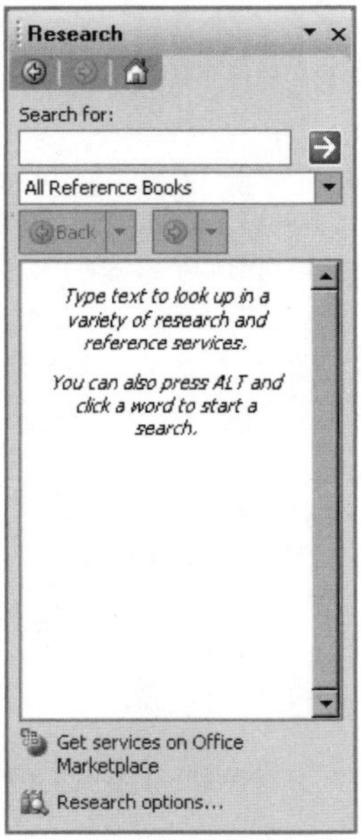

Exhibit 1-6: The Research task pane

To use the Research task pane:

1   Choose Tools, Research to open the Research task pane, shown in Exhibit 1-6.

2   In the Search for box, type the word that you want to find.

3   From the All Reference Books list, select the search category.

Do it!

C-2: Using the Research task pane

Here's how	Here's why
1 Choose **Tools**, **Research...**	To open the Research task pane.
2 In the Search for box, type **msft**	
3 Click the drop-down button in the All References Books list, as shown	

Search for:

msft

All Reference Books

All Reference Books
   Encarta Dictionary: English (North America)
   Encarta Dictionary: English (U.K.)
   Encarta Dictionary: French
   English (U.S.) to French (France)
   English (U.S.) to German (Germany)
   Translation
All Research Sites
   eLibrary
   MSN Search
   Factiva News Search
   Encarta Encyclopedia: English (North America)
All Business and Financial Sites
   Gale Company Profiles
   MSN Money Stock Quotes

Research options...

Your list of references may vary.

| Select **MSN Money Stock Quotes** | From the All Reference Books list. |

4 Click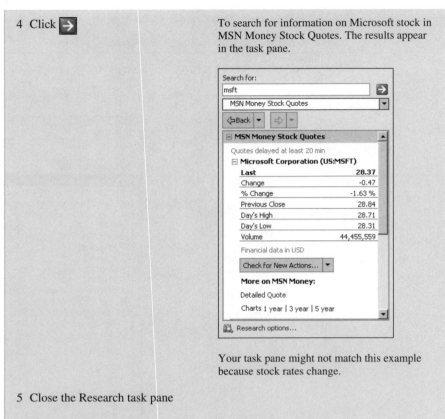

To search for information on Microsoft stock in MSN Money Stock Quotes. The results appear in the task pane.

Your task pane might not match this example because stock rates change.

5 Close the Research task pane

6 Close the document

If necessary.

Unit summary: Common features of Office 2003

Topic A

In this topic, you learned how to use **Assistance** to find additional help from the Microsoft Office Online site.

Topic B

In this topic, you learned how to download **additional templates** for Office 2003 applications by using the Microsoft Office Online Template site. You also learned how to download **additional clip art** by using the **Clip art on Office Online** option. You learned about **fax services** and how to use them to send faxes from within Word. You learned how to access **Web-based online services** and how to **download third-party software** from the Microsoft Office Online Office Marketplace Web page. You also learned how to search for Office updates by using the **Check for Updates** option.

Topic C

In this topic, you learned about **Instant Messaging**. You also learned how to use the **Research task pane**.

Independent practice activity

1 Display the New Document task pane.

2 Open the Microsoft Office Online Templates Web page.

3 Create a document based on the template Acknowledgement of Order. (*Hint:* This template is available in Letters to Customers under Marketing.)

4 Close the document without saving it.

5 Close the browser window.

6 Open Acknowledgement.

7 Save the document as **My acknowledgement**.

8 Open the Clip Art task pane.

9 Open the Microsoft Office Clip Art and Media Web page.

10 Download clip art of a globe. (*Hint:* Under BROWSE CLIP ART AND MEDIA, click Maps.)

11 Close the browser window.

12 Paste the clip art onto the rectangle in the upper-right corner of the document (search for "maps").

13 Using the Research task pane, find the meaning of the word **Expedite** in U.S. English.

14 Close the Research task pane.

15 Update and close the document.

Unit 2

New features in Word, Excel, and PowerPoint

Unit time: 90 minutes

Complete this unit, and you'll know how to:

A Use enhanced accessibility and readability features, insert voice comments, lock styles, and protect documents in Word 2003.

B Use lists and smart tags, and compare workbooks side by side in Excel 2003.

C Use smart tags, the Thesaurus, and the Package for CD features in PowerPoint 2003.

Topic A: New features in Word 2003

Explanation

Microsoft Word 2003 provides several new features to help you customize Word according to your preferences. The new features include:

- **Enhanced accessibility** — Features such as additional keyboard shortcuts make Word easier to use. For example, people with poor visibility can now use keyboard shortcuts to open, view, and explore Microsoft Office help.
- **Improved readability** — The new Reading Layout view makes it easier to read documents on screen. This view provides larger text, shorter lines, and pages that fit the screen.
- **Voice comments** — You can insert voice comments when reviewing a document (if you have a microphone).
- **Formatting restrictions** — You can restrict the use of formatting styles in a document.
- **Document protection** — You can protect documents from modification by specifying editing restrictions.

Accessibility

The accessibility features make it easier for a wide range of users, including those with physical disabilities, to access Word effectively. These features include expandable links and keyboard shortcuts that you can use in the Word Help task pane, the Help window, or the Ask a Question box.

You can use keyboard shortcuts to expand links in the Help window. When you expand a link, the help information about that topic appears in the current window (so you don't have to jump to a new page). To expand or collapse a specific link, use the left or right arrow keys. To expand or collapse all the links, click the Show All or Hide All links located at the top of the Help window.

The following table lists keyboard shortcuts for working in the Help system:

Shortcut	Description
F1	Displays the Word Help task pane.
F6	Switches between the Word Help task pane and the active application.
TAB	Selects the next item in the Word Help task pane or the next hyperlink in the Help window.
SHIFT + TAB	Selects the previous item in the Word Help task pane or the previous hyperlink in the Help window.
↵ ENTER	Expands the selected item in the Word Help task pane, Help window, or Ask a Question box.
↑ or ↓	Selects the previous or next items in the Table of Contents in the Word Help task pane or the Ask a Question box.

Shortcut	Description
⬅ or ➡	Expands or collapses the selected item in the Table of Contents in the Word Help task pane or the Ask a Question box.
ALT + ⬅	Moves to the previous task pane.
ALT + ➡	Moves to the next task pane.
CTRL + F1	Closes and opens the current task pane.
ALT + U	Tiles the Microsoft Word 2003 window with the Microsoft Office Word Help window.
CTRL + P	Prints the current topic of the Help window.

Exhibit 2-1: The Microsoft Office Word Help window

Do it!

A-1:   Using enhanced accessibility

Here's how	Here's why
1 Choose **Help**, **Microsoft Office Word Help**	To display the Word Help task pane.
2 Point as shown	**See also** ⬛ What's New The other links in the "See also" section are now visible.
3 Click as shown	**See also** ⬛ What's New ⬛ Contact Us ⬛ Accessibility Help ⬛ Online Content Settings... To open the Microsoft Office Word Help window, as shown in Exhibit 2-1.
4 Press (TAB)	☞ Show All The Show All link, located at the top of the Microsoft Office Word Help window, is selected, as shown here.
Press (TAB) two more times	▶ Keyboard shortcuts for using the **Help** task pane and Help window The "Keyboard shortcuts for using the Help task pane and Help window" link is selected, as shown here.
5 Press (↵ ENTER)	To expand the node.
Observe the keyboard shortcuts for using the Word Help task pane	
6 Press (ALT) + (U)	The Help window is tiled with the Word 2003 program window. If the Help window is already tiled, it will become untiled.
7 Close the Help window	
8 Close the Word Help task pane	Click the Close button in the upper-right corner of the task pane.

Reading Layout view

Explanation

Word 2003 makes it easier to read documents on your computer screen with the new Reading Layout view. This view hides the Standard and Formatting toolbars to provide more viewing space. This view also automatically scales the document to pages that fit neatly on screen. Reading Layout view also provides a Document Map and thumbnail images so you can quickly navigate to different sections of a document. You can also highlight and review documents in Reading Layout view.

To switch to this new view, choose View, Reading Layout, or click the Read button on the Standard toolbar. Exhibit 2-2 shows a document in Reading Layout view. In this view, the pages in the document are referred to as *screens*.

To view multiple pages, click the Allow Multiple Pages button on the Reading Layout toolbar. You can scroll down to view the other screens.

Reading Layout toolbar   Allow Multiple Pages button

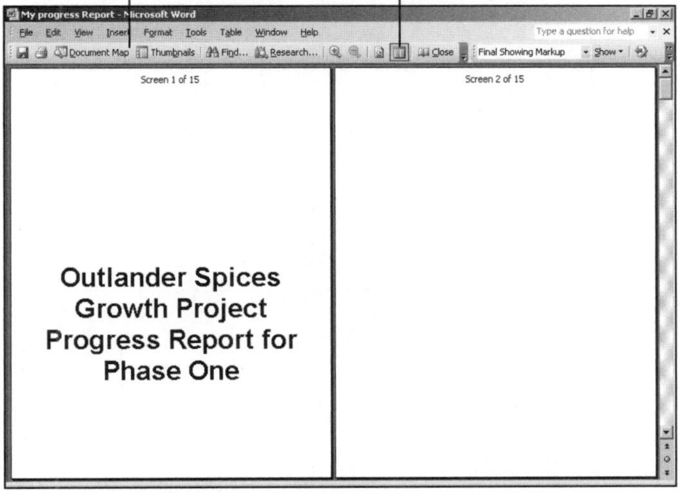

Exhibit 2-2: The Reading Layout view

Do it!

A-2:   Using Reading Layout view

Here's how	Here's why
1 Open Progress Report	From the current unit folder.
Save the document as **My progress report**	In the current unit folder.
2 Click [📖 Read]	(On the Standard toolbar. The Standard toolbar and the Formatting toolbar must be on separate lines for the Read button to be visible.) To switch to Reading Layout view. Multiple screens are available in this view.
3 Click [▼]	(In the lower-right part of the screen.) To view the next screen in the document along with the previous screen. Two screens—Screen 2 of 15 and Screen 3 of 15—appear in Reading Layout view.
4 Click [▣]	(The Allow Multiple Pages button is on the Reading Layout toolbar.) The first screen of the progress report document appears.
5 Click [Document Map]	(On the Reading Layout toolbar.) A list of the document's sections appears.
In the Document Map, click **Ann Salinski, VP Financial Services**	To jump to the section about Ann Salinski.
Click [Document Map]	To close the Document Map.
6 Click **Close**	(On the Reading Layout toolbar.) To switch to Normal view.
7 Update the document	

Voice comments

Explanation

You can insert voice comments while reviewing a document. For people who prefer to speak rather than type their comments, this is an effective way to review documents.

To insert a voice comment:

1 Select the text for which you want to insert the comment.
2 Display the Reviewing toolbar.
3 Click the Insert Voice button to open the Sound Recorder window.
4 In the Sound Recorder window, click the Record button.
5 Use a microphone to record the comment.
6 When finished, click the Stop button.

After recording, you can use Word 2003 to hear the comments. To do this:

1 On the Reviewing toolbar, click the Reviewing Pane button. The Reviewing pane appears.
2 Choose View, Print Layout to switch to Print Layout view.
3 Double-click the sound icon.

Do it!

A-3: Inserting voice comments

Here's how	Here's why
1 Select the text as shown	**Ann Salinski, VP Financial Services** Ann's role is to oversee the financials for this and has the final say on any cost overruns for (The text is in the second paragraph under the heading "The Project Team.") You'll insert a voice comment for this text.
2 Choose **View, Toolbars, Reviewing**	To display the Reviewing toolbar.
3 Click [icon]	Sound Object in My progress rep... File Edit Effects Help Position: 0.00 sec. Length: 0.00 sec. (The Insert Voice button is on the Reviewing toolbar.) The Reviewing pane appears at the bottom of the window. Also, a Sound Recorder window appears with the title "Sound Object in My progress report.doc." If a message box appears indicating that the printer has not responded, click Yes.

4 Click 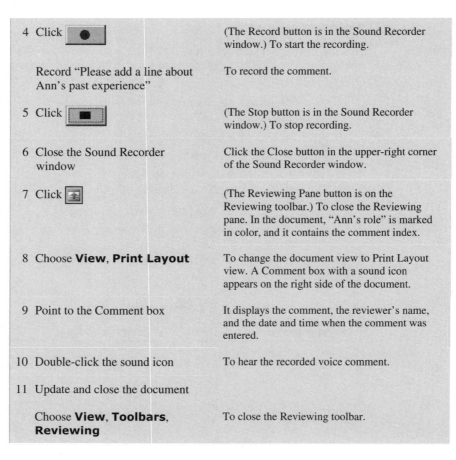	(The Record button is in the Sound Recorder window.) To start the recording.
Record "Please add a line about Ann's past experience"	To record the comment.
5 Click	(The Stop button is in the Sound Recorder window.) To stop recording.
6 Close the Sound Recorder window	Click the Close button in the upper-right corner of the Sound Recorder window.
7 Click	(The Reviewing Pane button is on the Reviewing toolbar.) To close the Reviewing pane. In the document, "Ann's role" is marked in color, and it contains the comment index.
8 Choose **View**, **Print Layout**	To change the document view to Print Layout view. A Comment box with a sound icon appears on the right side of the document.
9 Point to the Comment box	It displays the comment, the reviewer's name, and the date and time when the comment was entered.
10 Double-click the sound icon	To hear the recorded voice comment.
11 Update and close the document	
Choose **View**, **Toolbars**, **Reviewing**	To close the Reviewing toolbar.

Formatting restrictions

Explanation

One of the goals of Office 2003 is to support workgroup collaboration. If you're creating a document to be shared with others, you might need to consider document protection. You can protect a document from changes in formatting, content, or both.

When you apply formatting restrictions, the Formatting toolbar is disabled, and only the styles that you explicitly make available can be used. To apply formatting restrictions:

1 Choose Tools, Protect Document to open the Protect Document task pane.

2 Under Formatting restrictions, check Limit formatting to a selection of styles.

3 Click Settings to open the Formatting Restrictions dialog box. At the top of the dialog box, Limit formatting to a selection of styles should be checked.

4 You can specify four settings in the Checked styles are currently allowed list:

- **All** — Allow all listed styles to be applied in the document.

- **Recommended Minimum** — Allow the styles that Microsoft recommends and uses in a table of contents and for bulleted and numbered lists.

- **None** — Disables all styles.

- **User specified styles** — Allows all styles that the user checks in the list.

5 Click OK. A message box appears, indicating that the document might contain formatting or styles that are not allowed. You can click Yes to remove the formatting or styles, or No to ignore them.

6 Under Start enforcement, click the Yes, Start Enforcing Protection button to open the Start Enforcing Protection dialog box.

7 In the Enter new password (optional) box, type the password.

8 In the Reenter password to confirm box, type the password again.

9 Click OK. On the Formatting toolbar, all the options except the Style list are disabled.

To enable the buttons of the Formatting toolbar, you need to unprotect the template or document. To do so, display the Protect Document task pane, and click the Stop Protection button. When the Unprotect Document dialog box appears, type the password, and click OK. You can now modify the document as you wish and then restart the protection.

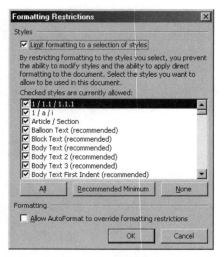

Exhibit 2-3: The Formatting Restrictions dialog box

Exhibit 2-4: The Start Enforcing Protection dialog box

Do it!

A-4: Applying formatting restrictions

Here's how	Here's why
1 Open Ann Salinski	
2 Save the document as **My ann salinski**	
3 Choose **Tools, Protect Document...**	To open the Protect Document task pane.
4 Under Formatting restrictions, check **Limit formatting to a selection of styles**	To specify the list of styles to be locked.

5 Under Formatting restrictions, click as shown	**Formatting restrictions** ☑ Limit formatting to a selection of styles Settings...
	To open the Formatting Restrictions dialog box, as shown in Exhibit 2-3. You can use this dialog box to specify the styles that need be locked.
6 Clear **Heading1 (recommended)**	To remove this style from the list.
7 Click **OK**	A message box appears.
8 Click **Yes**	To remove formatting from all text that uses the Heading1 style.
9 In the Protect Document task pane, click **Yes, Start Enforcing Protection**	To open the Start Enforcing Protection dialog box, as shown in Exhibit 2-4.
10 In the Enter new password (optional) box, type **password**	You'll protect the document by using this password.
In the Reenter password to confirm box, type **password**	
Click **OK**	To close the Start Enforcing Protection dialog box and apply the password settings.
11 Observe the Formatting toolbar	On the Formatting toolbar, all the options except for the Style list are disabled.
12 In the Protect Document task pane, click **Stop Protection**	To open the Unprotect Document dialog box. You'll unprotect the document to use the Formatting toolbar.
In the Password box, type **password**	
Click **OK**	To close the Unprotect Document dialog box and unprotect the document.
13 Observe the Formatting toolbar	The options on the Formatting toolbar are now enabled.
14 Update the document	

Document protection

Another consideration when sharing documents is deciding who will have access to them. In Word 2003, you can protect documents from unauthorized users by specifying a password. This means that you need to enter that password to unprotect the document when you need to edit it.

To protect a document:

1 Open the Protect Document task pane.

2 Under Editing restrictions, check Allow only this type of editing in the document.

3 From the list under Editing restrictions, select Tracked changes.

4 Under Start enforcement, click the Yes, Start Enforcing Protection button. The Start Enforcing Protection dialog box opens.

5 Enter and confirm the password in the Enter new password (optional) and Reenter password to confirm boxes.

6 Click OK.

When you protect a document with a password, you can make changes, but you cannot accept or reject tracked changes. If you want to accept or reject the changes in a protected document, you need to unprotect it. To do so, open the Unprotect Document dialog box by choosing Tools, Unprotect Document, and specify the password. Click OK.

A-5: Protecting a document

Here's how	Here's why
1 Under Editing restrictions, check **Allow only this type of editing in the document**	(In the Protect Document task pane.) To specify the type of editing restrictions.
From the list under Editing restrictions, select **Tracked changes**	To ensure that users can make changes but cannot reject or accept changes.
2 Under Start enforcement, click **Yes, Start Enforcing Protection**	To open the Start Enforcing Protection dialog box.
3 In the Enter new password (optional) box, type **password**	You'll protect the document by using this password.
In the Reenter password to confirm box, type **password**	
4 Click **OK**	To close the Start Enforcing Protection dialog box and to apply the password settings.

5 Under the heading "The Project team," change **outside** to **external**	In the first sentence of the first paragraph under the heading "The Project team."
6 Observe the Reviewing toolbar	The Accept Change and the Reject Change/Delete Comment buttons are disabled. This means that you can't accept or reject changes made in the document.
7 Open the Unprotect Document dialog box	(Click the Stop Protection button in the Protect Document task pane.) You need to unprotect the document to accept or reject the changes.
In the Password box, type **password**	
Click **OK**	To close the Unprotect Document dialog box and to unprotect the document.
8 Click as shown	
	(The Accept Change button is on the Reviewing toolbar.) A menu appears.
Choose **Accept All Changes in Document**	To accept all the changes in the document.
Close the Protect Document task pane	
9 Update and close the document	
10 Close Word	

Topic B: New features in Excel 2003

Explanation

Microsoft Excel 2003 provides several new worksheet features to help you work more efficiently. You can manage and analyze data more easily by using improvements in list functionality. Smart tags are more flexible. You can use them to link cell contents with other applications, such as Outlook. You can also use the Compare Side by Side option to examine two workbooks simultaneously.

Creating lists

By designating a range as a list, you can work with the data in that list independently of the data outside the list. Functions such as filtering and sorting data are more readily available, making it much more efficient to manipulate and analyze information.

To create a list:

1 Select the range that you want to designate as a list.
2 Choose Data, List, Create List.
3 You will be prompted to specify the data for your list. If you've already selected the data, click OK.
4 If your data selection includes headers (column or row headings), then check My list has headers.
5 Click OK.

Filtering and sorting lists

After data has been designated as a list, column headings automatically display AutoFilters. You can use these filters to analyze the list by displaying only the data that meets certain criteria. Included in the AutoFilter list are sorting options. You can sort the list in ascending or descending order.

When you designate a range as a list, common aggregate functions used for data analysis, such as Sum, Average, and Standard Deviation, are more readily available. You can add a total row to a list by choosing Data, List, Total Row.

Do it!

B-1: Working with lists

Here's how	Here's why
1 Start Microsoft Office Excel 2003	Click Start, and choose Programs, Microsoft Office, Microsoft Office Excel 2003.
2 Open Employee Information	
Save the workbook as **My employee information**	
3 Select A3:F22	To select the cells that will be included in the list. This range is only a subset of the data in this worksheet. The data continues through row 44, but the list will include only data through row 22.
4 Choose **Data, List, Create List...**	To open the Create List dialog box.
Verify that **My list has headers** is selected	To indicate that the column headings were included in the list range.
Click **OK**	To create the list.
5 Click any cell in the list	To select the list. A blue border surrounds the list, and each column heading has an AutoFilter. The asterisk (*) at the bottom of the list designates the row where new list entries can be added.
6 Click the Department AutoFilter arrow	To display the list of Department filter criteria.
Select **Human resources**	To display only those employees in the Human Resources department. Notice that the list is filtered independently of the rest of the data. The data in rows 24 through 44 remain unaffected by the filtering process.

7 Display all employees in the list	Click the Department AutoFilter arrow and then select (All).
8 Click the Region AutoFilter arrow	To display the list of Region filter criteria.
9 Select **Sort Ascending**	To sort the list in ascending order by region.
10 Select any cell within the list	To select the list. Notice that row 23 is available for a new entry within the list.
Select F23	
Choose **Data**, **List**, **Total Row**	To sum the earnings for all employees in the list.
11 Click as shown	2332850
	To display other common statistical functions.
12 Select **Average**	To display the average earnings of all employees in the list.
13 Update the file	
Close the file	

Using the Date smart tag

Explanation

Excel provides several built-in smart tags, which recognize and label data as a particular type. For example, data recognized as a date will display a Date smart tag. You can use smart tags to link cell contents with other applications, such as Outlook. So, for example, if you have a cell containing a date, you can use the Date smart tag to link the cell content to Outlook. You can then create meeting schedules and specify tasks to be performed on the selected date.

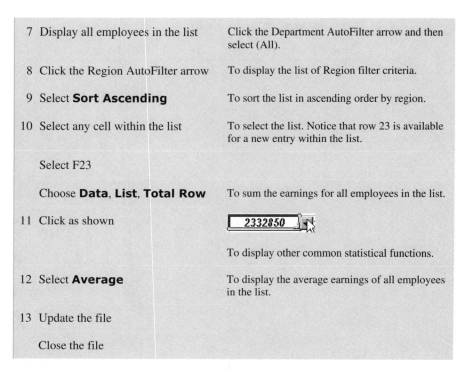

Exhibit 2-5: The Untitled – Meeting window

Do it!   ### B-2:   Using the Date smart tag

Here's how	Here's why
1 Open Stock Details	
2 Save the workbook as **My stock details**	
3 Choose **Tools, AutoCorrect Options...**	To open the AutoCorrect: English (U.S.) dialog box.
Activate the Smart Tags tab	
4 Check **Label data with smart tags**	(If necessary.) To activate the smart tags options.
5 Under Recognizers, check **Date** and check **Financial Symbol**	(If necessary.) To activate the Date and Financial Symbol smart tag lists.
Click **OK**	To apply the changes. The Date smart tag appears in the cell C5.
6 Click as shown	The Smart Tag Actions menu appears.
Observe the menu	The menu contains smart tag actions, such as Schedule a Meeting and Show My Calendar. You can choose these options to schedule meetings and set daily schedules.
Select **Schedule a Meeting**	The Untitled – Meeting window appears, as shown in Exhibit 2-5. You can use this window to send a meeting invitation to your co-workers.
7 Choose **File, Close**	To close the Untitled – Meeting window.
Click **No**	

Compare workbooks side by side

Using a single workbook to review changes made by multiple users can be challenging. With the new Compare Side by Side feature, you can examine differences between two workbooks by scrolling through the workbooks simultaneously to identify differences. This approach can be easier and more convenient than merging all the changes into a single workbook for examination.

Do it!

B-3:   Comparing workbooks side by side

Here's how	Here's why
1 Open Q4 Stock Details	
2 Choose **Window**, **Compare Side by Side with My stock details**	The two workbooks are tiled vertically with Q4 Stock Details displayed above My stock details.
3 In the Q4 Stock Details window, scroll down	The My stock details window scrolls as well. This enables you to compare the two workbooks row by row. The companies and company codes are the same, but there are different dates and stock values.
4 In the Compare Side by Side toolbar, click **Close Side by Side**	To close the comparison view.
5 Close the workbooks	Don't save changes.
6 Close Excel	

Topic C: New features in PowerPoint 2003

Explanation

In Microsoft PowerPoint 2003, smart tags and appearance improvements make it easier to view and create presentations. You can also easily package presentations in a CD format.

Smart tags

You can use smart tags to obtain data related to specific information. For example, if you type the date on a slide, you can view that day's appointments in the Outlook window.

Do it!

C-1: Using smart tags

Here's how	Here's why
1 Start Microsoft Office PowerPoint 2003	Click Start, and choose Programs, Microsoft Office, Microsoft Office PowerPoint 2003.
2 Open Outlander	
Save the presentation as **My outlander**	
3 Move to the fourth slide in the presentation	
4 Choose **Tools**, **AutoCorrect Options...**	To open the AutoCorrect: English (U.S.) dialog box. You'll select the smart tags that might appear in the document.
Activate the Smart Tags tab	If necessary.
Check **Label text with smart tags**	If necessary.
Under Recognizers, verify that Date is checked	
5 Click **OK**	To apply the changes.
6 In slide four, click as shown	**Performance**ⅈ
	To select the placeholder.
7 Press ⌷SPACEBAR	
Type **on 02/03/2005**	To complete the slide title.
8 Deselect the placeholder	Click anywhere on the slide outside the placeholder.

9	Display the Smart Tags Actions menu	Point to the date you entered, and click the down arrow on the Smart Tags Actions button.	
10	Choose **Show my Calendar**	(The Calendar window appears for the date you entered.) You'll specify the time of the meeting on the specified date.	
11	Click as shown	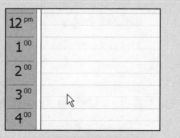	
12	Type **Monthly meeting** Close the Calendar window	To schedule a meeting at 3 P.M. on 02/03/2005.	
13	Display the Calendar window	(Choose Show my Calendar from the Smart Tags Actions menu.) The meeting has been scheduled for 3 P.M.	
14	Close the Calendar window		
15	Update the presentation		

The Thesaurus

Explanation

The new Research task pane provides access to a variety of reference information and resources, including a Thesaurus. You can check for synonyms of words in a presentation by using the Thesaurus. You can also replace a looked-up word with any of the synonyms.

Do it!

C-2: Using the Thesaurus

Here's how	Here's why
1 Move to the second slide in the presentation	This is the slide titled "Project justification."
2 Select **inventory**	You'll replace this word with a synonym.

3 Choose **Tools, Thesaurus...**

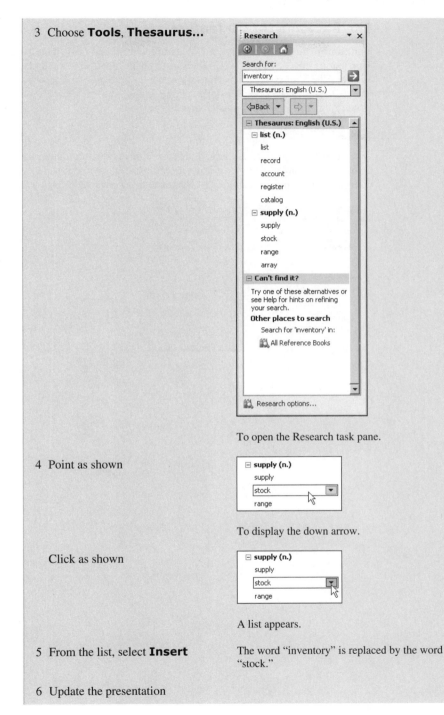

To open the Research task pane.

4 Point as shown

To display the down arrow.

Click as shown

A list appears.

5 From the list, select **Insert**

The word "inventory" is replaced by the word "stock."

6 Update the presentation

The Package for CD feature

You can use the new Package for CD feature to efficiently distribute your presentations. This feature copies your PowerPoint files to a CD, along with the updated PowerPoint Viewer. The Viewer enables you to show the presentation on a computer that does not have Microsoft PowerPoint installed. Improvements to the Viewer include support of PowerPoint 2003 graphics, media, and animations.

Packaging presentations

When you package a presentation to display it on another computer, the destination computer does not have to have PowerPoint installed. You can use the Viewer to run your presentation. (You cannot, however, use the Viewer to change a presentation.)

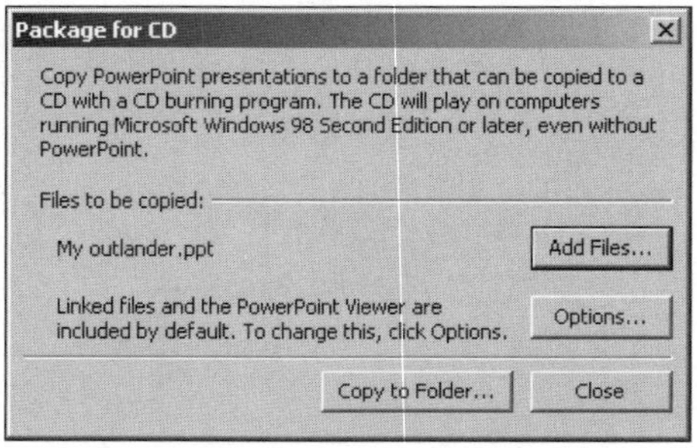

Exhibit 2-6: The Package for CD dialog box

Do it!

C-3: Packaging a presentation

Here's how	Here's why
1 Choose **File**, **Package for CD...**	To open the Package for CD dialog box, shown in Exhibit 2-6. (If you don't have a CD burning program on your computer, this dialog box will look slightly different.)
2 Click **Options**	To open the Options dialog box.
3 Clear **Linked files**	This option isn't necessary because the current presentation does not contain any linked files.
Check **Embedded TrueType fonts**	To embed all the TrueType fonts used in the presentation.
Click **OK**	To close the Options dialog box and return to the Package for CD dialog box.
4 Click **Copy to Folder**	To open the Copy to Folder dialog box.
Verify that the Folder name box reads PresentationCD	
Click **Browse**	To open the Choose Location dialog box. You'll specify a path to save the packaged presentation.
5 Navigate to the current unit folder	
Double-click **Package**	To open the Package folder.
Click **Select**	To close the Copy to Folder dialog box. The Location box contains the name of the current folder.
Click **OK**	A status box appears, showing the progress of the file compression.
6 Click **Close**	To close the Package for CD dialog box.
7 Update and close the presentation	
8 Close PowerPoint	

Unit summary: New features in Word, Excel, and PowerPoint

Topic A   In this topic, you learned about the **accessibility** features in Word 2003. You also learned how to **switch** to **Reading Layout view** by using the **Read button** on the Standard toolbar. In addition, you learned how to **insert voice comments** by using the **Reviewing toolbar**. You also learned how to **restrict formatting styles** and **protect documents** by using the **Protect Document task pane**.

Topic B   In this topic, you learned how to **apply a smart tag** to cells in Excel 2003. You learned that you can apply a smart tag by selecting the Smart Tags option in the AutoCorrect dialog box and selecting a smart tag from the Smart Tags Actions menu.

Topic C   In this topic, you learned how to use a **smart tag** in PowerPoint 2003. You also learned how to use the **Thesaurus**, and you learned how to **package a presentation** for a CD.

Independent practice activity

1 Open Word. Display the Word Help task pane by using the keyboard shortcut.

2 View help on mail merge data sources.

3 Click **About mail merge data sources**.

4 Observe the help on mail merge data sources.

5 Close the Help window.

6 Open Plan.

7 Save the document as **My plan** in the current unit folder.

8 View the document in Reading Layout view.

9 Switch back to Normal view.

10 Under "The Project Team," select **four outside consultants**, and insert the following voice comment: "The outside consultants are hired on a contract basis."

11 Listen to the recorded comment.

12 Update and close the document.

13 Close Word.

14 Open Excel.

15 Enter **02/03/2005** in any cell of the workbook.

16 Save the workbook as **My excel smart tag** in the current unit folder.

17 Check the schedule for 02/03/2005 by using a smart tag. (*Hint:* Choose Show my Calendar from the Smart Tags Actions menu. After checking, close the Calendar window.)

18 Close the workbook.

19 Close Excel.

20 Open PowerPoint.

21 Open Initiatives.

22 Save the presentation as **My initiatives**.

23 In the second slide, replace **company** with **corporation** by using the Thesaurus.

24 Package the presentation in the Practice Package folder. (*Hint:* The Practice Package folder is in the current unit folder. Under Options, Linked files should be clear and Embedded TrueType fonts should be checked.)

25 Update and close the presentation.

26 Close PowerPoint.

Unit 3

New features in Access and Outlook

Unit time: 90 minutes

Complete this unit, and you'll know how to:

A Set smart tags, inherit properties, view database object dependencies, back up a database, check for errors in forms, and get context-sensitive help in Access 2003.

B Create and use a search folder, add a flag to a message, examine the Junk E-mail Filter, and integrate the Calendar with other components in Outlook 2003.

Topic A: What's new in Access 2003

Explanation

The following are some of the new features in Access 2003:

- The Smart Tags property
- Property inheritance propagation
- Database object dependencies
- Database backup
- Error checking
- Context-sensitive help

The Smart Tags property

You can link Access to other Office applications, such as Outlook, by setting the Smart Tags property in Access database fields. Smart tags help you perform certain actions, such as sending e-mail and scheduling a meeting.

To set a smart tag for a field:

1   Open the table in Design view.
2   Display the general properties of the field.
3   Place the insertion point in the Smart Tags property box.
4   Click the Build button next to the Smart Tags property box to open the Smart Tags dialog box, shown in Exhibit 3-1. The Smart Tags dialog box displays the available smart tags.
5   Check the relevant smart tag.
6   Click OK to close the Smart Tags dialog box.

After setting a smart tag, you can use it to link to other Office applications. For example, if you set a smart tag for the name of a person, you can send e-mail directly to that person by using Outlook through Access. To do this:

1   Point to the field where you've set the smart tag.
2   Click the smart tag. The Smart Tag Actions menu appears.
3   Choose Send Mail to open a new Message window.
4   Specify the details of the message, and click Send.

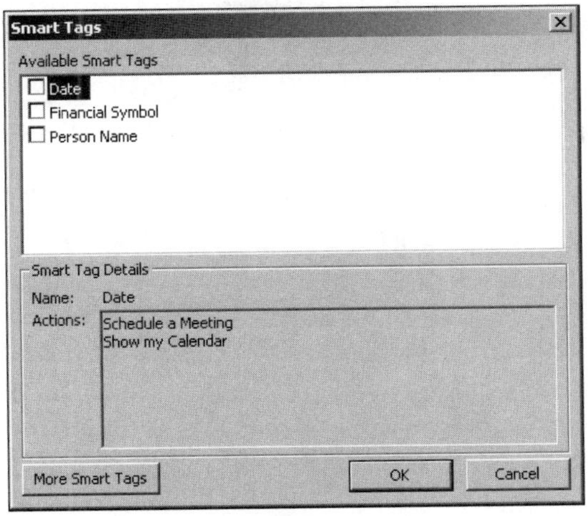

Exhibit 3-1: The Smart Tags dialog box

Do it!

A-1: Setting smart tags

Here's how	Here's why
1 Start Microsoft Office Access 2003	Click Start, and then choose Programs, Microsoft Office, Microsoft Office Access 2003.
2 Open DataEntryRules	From the current unit folder. If a security warning appears, click Yes and then click Open.
3 Open tblRetailer in Design view	You'll set a smart tag for the Last Name field so that you can send instant messages through Outlook from Access.
4 Display the general properties for the field strLastName	In the Field Name column, click on strLastName.
5 Click as shown	Smart Tags [_____]
6 **Click** [...]	(The Build button is located next to the Smart Tags property box.) To open the Smart Tags dialog box, shown in Exhibit 3-1.
7 Check **Person Name**	You will send e-mail based on the person's name.
Click **OK**	To close the Smart Tags dialog box. The general properties of the smart tag you specified, Person Name, appear in the Smart Tags property box.
8 Update the table	On the Standard toolbar, click the Save button.
9 Choose **View**, **Datasheet View**	Last Name Murray Schaaf Rivet Coleman Gordon Mager MacKenzie Willis Cruise Wilkins Roslyn Goldberg O'Halloran To switch to Datasheet view. A small triangle appears in the corner of the Last Name field. This indicates that you have set the Smart Tags property for this field.

10 Point as shown

Last Name	Phone
Murray	ⓘ 2) 665-4500 x123
Schaaf	(624) 390-8944

To display the smart tag.

Click as shown

Last Name	Phone
Murray	ⓘ 665-4500 x123
Schaaf	(624) 390-8944
Rivet	(523) Smart Tag Actions

The Smart Tag Actions menu appears.

Observe the Smart Tag Actions menu

Person Name: Murray
Send Mail
Schedule a Meeting
Open Contact
Add to Contacts

You can choose any of these actions.

Press [ESC]

To close the menu.

11 Close the table

12 Close DataEntryRules

Propagating inherited properties

Explanation

The property propagation feature enables objects, such as forms, to inherit the properties of their parent object. A *parent object* is an object, such as a table, on which various child objects are based. For example, you can create a form based on the data in a table. In this case, the table is the parent object, and the form is dependent on the table's properties. Any changes that you make in the table' format need to be reflected in the form as well. You can do this by using the propagation feature.

Do it!

A-2:   Inheriting properties

Here's how	Here's why
1 Open CreateForm	If a security warning appears, click Yes and then click Open.
2 In the Objects bar, click **Forms**	If necessary.
Open frmOrder	The date in the Order Date field is in the General Date format, 1/6/2004.
3 Close the form window	
4 In the Objects bar, click **Tables**	
Open tblOrder in Design view	
5 Display the general properties for the field dtmOrdDate	
From the Format list, select **Medium Date**	To apply this format to the date. The Property Update Options smart tag appears.
6 Click as shown	
7 Choose **Update Format everywhere dtmOrdDate is used**	The Update Properties dialog box opens. The dialog box lists the names of all the objects that contain the dtmOrdDate field. The form frmOrder is the only object that contains that field.
Click **Yes**	To close the dialog box and to update the format of the dtmOrdDate field.
8 Update and close the table	
9 In the Objects bar, click **Forms**	
Open frmOrder	The format of the date in the Order Date field has changed to Medium Date.
10 Close the form window	

Database object dependencies

Explanation

You might need to relate various objects in a database to each other. These related objects are dependent on each other. For example, if you relate a form to a table, the form is dependent on the table. When you delete the table, the relationship with the form is lost, and the form might not work properly. So, before deleting an object, you must know what its dependent objects are.

To view all the object dependencies in a database:

1 Open the database.

2 Select the object.

3 Choose View, Object Dependencies. The Object Dependencies task pane appears, showing the relationships for the selected object.

Do it!

A-3:   Viewing database object dependencies

Here's how	Here's why
1 In the Objects bar, click **Tables**	
2 Select **tblOrder**	(If necessary.) You'll view the object dependencies of this table.
3 Choose **View**, **Object Dependencies...**	To display the Object Dependencies task pane. The objects that depend on the table tblOrder appear in the task pane. The form frmOrder is the only dependent of the table tblOrder.
4 Close the Object Dependencies task pane	

Database backup

Explanation

When your database is corrupted due to a virus attack or power failure, for example, you might lose some or all of your data. There should be some safeguard to prevent this. Access provides a safeguard by which you can save a copy of your database in some other location. Then you can retrieve the data even if your original database is corrupted.

To back up a database:

1 Open the database that you want to back up.
2 Choose File, Back Up Database to open the Save Backup As dialog box.
3 Enter a name for the backup database.
4 Click Save to make a backup copy of the database.

Do it!

A-4:   Creating a database backup

Here's how	Here's why
1 Choose **File**, **Back Up Database...**	To open the Save Backup As dialog box. You'll make a backup copy of the CreateForm database.
Edit the File name box to read **CreateForm Backup**	
2 Click **Save**	To close the Save Backup As dialog box and to save the backup copy of the database. The status bar first shows the progress of the backup and then displays "Ready."
3 Close CreateForm	
4 Open CreateForm Backup	(If a security warning appears, click Yes and then click Open.) The CreateForm Backup database contains all of the tables that are in the CreateForm database.
5 In the Objects bar, click **Forms**	The CreateForm Backup database contains the same forms as the CreateForm database.
6 Close CreateForm Backup	

Checking for errors

Explanation

You can set Access to automatically check for errors in forms. When you check for errors, the Trace Error button appears next to those controls that have an error value. This helps you identify the errors. Access also provides options for fixing the detected errors. You can click the Error Checking Options button to correct or ignore these errors.

The following list identifies the types of errors along with the situations in which they occur:

- **Unassociated label and control** — Occurs when you select a label and a control that are not associated with each other.
- **New unassociated labels** — Occurs when you add a label to a form or report and the label is not associated with any other control.
- **Keyboard shortcut errors** — Occurs when you select a control with an invalid shortcut key.
- **Invalid control properties** — Occurs when you select a control with one or more properties set to invalid values.
- **Common report errors** — Occurs when your report either has an invalid sorting and grouping definition or is wider than the selected paper size.

Do it!

A-5:   Checking for errors in forms

Here's how	Here's why
1 Open AdvancedForms	If a security warning appears, click Yes and then click Open.
2 Open frmRetailer in Design view	
3 Observe the labels Retailer ID and Retailer Name	Retailer ID Retailer Name (You might need to move the Toolbox to view these labels.) There is a green error indicator in the upper-left corner of these labels. This indicates that the labels contain errors. These types of errors occur when the same access key (shortcut key) is specified for more than one control on the same form.
4 Display the property sheet for the label control Retailer ID	Right-click the label, and choose Properties.
Activate the Format tab	If necessary.
Observe the Caption box	The "&" before "Retailer ID" implies that "R" is the access key for the Retailer ID label.
Close the property sheet	

5   Display the property sheet for the
    label control Retailer Name

    Observe the Caption box   The "&" before "Retailer Name" indicates that
                                            "R" is the access key for this label also. This is
                                            the reason for the error in the labels.

    Close the property sheet

6   Click 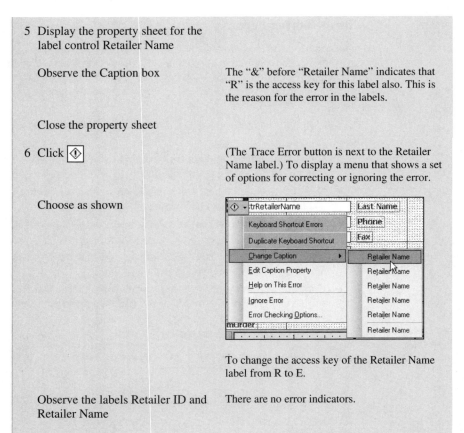   (The Trace Error button is next to the Retailer
                                            Name label.) To display a menu that shows a set
                                            of options for correcting or ignoring the error.

    Choose as shown

    To change the access key of the Retailer Name
    label from R to E.

    Observe the labels Retailer ID and   There are no error indicators.
    Retailer Name

7   Update and close the form

Context-sensitive help

Explanation   As you are working with SQL queries, you may have questions about the statements
within the queries. In Access, you can get help on specific SQL statements directly
while you're working. For example, if you're working with a SELECT statement and
you don't remember the syntax, you can get help without leaving the query.

To obtain help about a specific SQL statement:

1   Open the table.
2   Switch to SQL View.
3   Select the statement on which you need help.
4   Press F1.

Do it!   **A-6:   Getting context-sensitive help**

Here's how	Here's why
1 In the Objects bar, click **Queries**	
2 Open qryRetailerOrder in Design view	
Click as shown	
	(On the Query Design toolbar.) A menu appears.
Choose **SQL View**	To switch to SQL view.
3 Place the insertion point on the SELECT command	You'll check the syntax of this command.
4 Press F1	To open the Microsoft Office Access Help window. The window displays the syntax of the SELECT statement and describes the different parts of the SELECT statement.
Close the Microsoft Office Access Help window	
5 Place the insertion point in the ON keyword	You'll check the syntax of this clause.
6 Press F1	To open the Microsoft Office Access Help window. The window now displays information related to the ON clause.
Close the Microsoft Office Access Help window	
7 Close the qryRetailerOrder : Select Query window	
8 Close AdvancedForms	
9 Close Access	

Topic B: What's new in Outlook 2003

Explanation

Microsoft Outlook 2003 has several new features, including search folders, Quick Flags, a Junk E-mail Filter, and provisions for integrating the Calendar with other features in Outlook. You use search folders to access your e-mail based on search conditions. Quick Flags and a new Junk E-mail Filter help you better organize and screen your e-mail messages. You can also integrate the Calendar with other Outlook features, such as Contacts, to track and schedule activities.

Search folders

You can use *search folders* to view e-mail by category. Search folders are virtual folders. They do not physically contain messages; rather, they provide views of only those messages that meet specified criteria. For example, you can create a search folder to view all e-mail containing the text "Welcome."

To create a search folder:

1 In the Navigation pane, right-click Search Folders.
2 Choose New Search Folder to open the New Search Folder dialog box.
3 From the Select a Search Folder list, select a condition.
4 Click OK.

Do it!

B-1: Creating and using a search folder

Here's how	Here's why
1 Start Microsoft Office Outlook 2003	Click Start, and then choose Programs, Microsoft Office, Microsoft Office Outlook 2003. If necessary, maximize the Outlook window.
2 In the Navigation pane, right-click **Search Folders**	A shortcut menu appears.
Choose **New Search Folder...**	To open the New Search Folder dialog box.
3 Under Organizing Mail, select **Mail with specific words**	To specify the condition.
Click **Choose**	To open the Search Text dialog box.
4 In the box, type as shown	Specify words or phrases to search for in the subject or body: Sales report To search for e-mail with the text "Sales report" in the Subject field or message body.
Click **Add**	The text "Sales report" is added to the Search list.
Click **OK**	To close the Search Text dialog box.

5	Click **OK**	To close the New Search Folder dialog box. In the Navigation pane, under Search Folders, a new folder named "Containing Sales report" appears. All e-mail containing the text "sales report" can be viewed through this new folder.
6	Open the Inbox folder	
7	Create a new message	Click the New button on the Standard toolbar.
8	Address the message to your partner	In the To box, type the name of your partner.
	In the Subject box, type **Sales report of the western region**	
	In the Message body, type **Chamomile Flowers $100** **Chili Pepper Powder $255**	
9	Send the message	Click Send.
10	Expand Search Folders	(If necessary. Click the plus sign near Search Folders.) The search folder you created appears in the Navigation pane.
11	Open the **Containing Sales report (1)** folder	(Click Containing Sales report in the Navigation pane.) To view the contents of the folder. A new message, with the words "Sales report" in the Subject field, appears in the Folder Contents list. The new message, with the term "Sales report" in the subject, appears in the Folder Contents list.
12	Open the message with the subject "Sales report of the western region"	(Double-click the message in the Folder Contents list.) To read the contents of the message.
	Close the message window	

Quick Flags

Explanation

In Outlook 2003, you can quickly flag an e-mail message for follow-up by clicking the flag icon next to the message. Several flag colors are available to help you categorize and find messages more easily. When you flag an item for follow-up, it's automatically placed in the For Follow Up search folder.

Do it!

B-2: Assigning a flag to a message

Here's how	Here's why
1 In the Navigation pane, click **Inbox**	To display all the messages in the Inbox. To the right of each message, a flag icon appears.
2 Right-click the flag icon on the message of your choice	⚑ Red Flag ⚑ Blue Flag ⚑ Yellow Flag ⚑ Green Flag ⚑ Orange Flag ⚑ Purple Flag ✓ Flag Complete Add Reminder... Clear Flag Set Default Flag ▶ A shortcut menu appears. Several flag colors are available if you want to categorize your messages by flag color.
3 Select a flag	To automatically place the message in the For Follow Up search folder.

The Junk E-mail Filter

Explanation

Using state-of-the-art technology, the new Junk E-mail Filter examines your incoming e-mail messages. It reviews the message subject and body for indications that the message is junk mail. Any message identified as possible junk mail is then automatically placed in a special Junk E-mail folder, where you can read it later at your convenience.

You can assist the filter in finding junk e-mail by using *filter lists*. Three filter lists are available:

- **Safe Senders List** — E-mail addresses that you include in this list will not be identified as junk mail. For example, if the Junk E-mail Filter incorrectly identifies a message as junk e-mail, you can add the sender's address to this list.

- **Safe Recipients List** — E-mail addresses that you send messages to will not be treated as junk mail if they are included in this list. For example, if you belong to mailing or distribution lists, you may want to add those names to this list.

- **Block Senders List** — E-mail addresses that you include in this list will automatically be treated as junk mail regardless of content.

By default, the Junk E-mail Filter is turned on and its protection level is set to Low. You can change the protection level. To do so:

1 Choose Tools, Options to open the Options dialog box.

2 Click Junk E-mail.

3 Select the desired protection level.

- No Automatic Filtering — Provides no junk e-mail protection.

- Low — Detects only obvious junk e-mail.

- High — Provides more protection.

- Safe Lists Only — Considers all messages to be junk e-mail, except for messages from addresses you specify in the Safe Senders or Safe Recipients lists.

4 If you want to immediately delete messages identified as possible junk e-mail, without saving them for later review, check the "Permanently delete suspected junk e-mail instead of moving it to the Junk E-mail folder" option.

5 Click OK to close the Junk E-mail Options dialog box.

6 Click OK to close the Options dialog box.

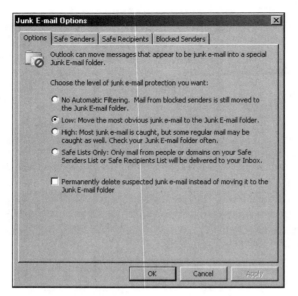

Exhibit 3-2: The Junk E-mail Options dialog box

Do it!

B-3:   Examining the Junk E-mail Filter

Here's how	Here's why
1 Choose **Tools**, **Options...**	The Options dialog box opens.
2 Click **Junk E-mail**	The Junk E-mail Options dialog box opens.
3 Examine the different levels of protection available	The default protection level is Low. Only messages that are obviously junk mail will be moved to the Junk E-mail folder.
4 Activate Safe Senders	Add e-mail addresses or domain names to this list if you never want them identified as junk mail. If you have a list of these addresses already compiled, you can import it to Outlook by using the Import from File button.
5 Activate Safe Recipients	Add e-mail addresses or domain names to this list if you never want mail sent to these addresses identified as junk mail.
6 Activate Blocked Senders	Add e-mail addresses or domain names to this list if you always want them identified as junk mail.
7 Click **Cancel**	To close the Junk E-mail Options dialog box.
Click **Cancel**	To close the Options dialog box.

Integrating the Calendar with other Outlook components

Explanation   The Calendar provides scheduling features in Outlook. For example, if you link a meeting request with a contact, you can easily track which person the meeting request is connected to. You can integrate the Calendar with other Outlook items, such as messages and tasks.

To integrate the Calendar with other Outlook items:

1   Activate the Calendar.
2   Create a new appointment.
3   Schedule the new appointment, and link categories or contacts with the appointment.
4   Save the appointment.

Do it!   ### B-4:   Integrating the Calendar with Contacts

Here's how	Here's why
1 Activate Calendar	You'll link a Calendar item to a contact.
Click **7 Week**	(If necessary.) To switch to Week view.
Select the next workday	In the Calendar pane.
2 Create a new appointment	(Choose Actions, New Appointment.) The Appointment dialog box opens.
In the Subject box, type **Marketing Meeting**	
Click **Contacts**	To open the Select Contacts dialog box. You can view the details of your contacts here.
From the Items list, select **Lee**, **Davis**	
3 Click **OK**	To close the Select Contacts dialog box. The contact Davis Lee appears in the box near the Contacts button.
4 Save and close the appointment	Click Save and Close.
5 Activate Contacts	
Open the contact **Lee, Davis**	(Double-click it.) You'll check whether the Calendar item has been linked with the contact.
Click the **Activities** tab	The appointment appears in the list, indicating that the Calendar item is now linked to the contact.
Save and close the contact	

Unit summary: New features in Access and Outlook

Topic A   In this topic, you learned about the **Smart Tags property**. You also learned about the **property propagation** feature. In addition, you learned about **database object dependencies**, and you learned how to **back up a database**. You learned how to **check for errors in forms**.

Topic B   In this topic, you learned how to use **search folders** in Outlook 2003. You flagged a message for follow-up and examined the new Junk E-mail Filter. You also learned how to **integrate calendar and contact information**.

Independent practice activity

1. Start Access.

2. Open DefiningDataEntryRules.

3. Open tblRetailer in Design view.

4. Set a smart tag for the strFirstName field. (*Hint:* Place the insertion point in strFirstName. Then, in the Smart Tags dialog box, click the Build button, check Person Name, and click OK.)

5. Update and close tblRetailer.

6. In the tblOrder table, change the date format of the dtmOrdDate field to Long Date. (*Hint:* Click the date field, and select the date format from the Format list.)

7. Update and close the table.

8. Create a backup for DefiningDataEntryRules, and name it **My DefiningDataEntryRules**.

9. Close DefiningDataEntryRules.

10. Close Access.

11. Start Outlook.

12. Send a message to your partner with the subject **Sales report for the eastern region**, and use the search folder to view the message.

13. Close Outlook.

Unit 4

XML and Office 2003

Unit time: 90 minutes

Complete this unit, and you'll know how to:

A Use XML in Access 2003.

B Use XML in Excel 2003.

C Use XML in Word 2003.

Topic A: XML and Access 2003

Explanation

Extensible Markup Language, or *XML*, is one of the most powerful emerging technologies used worldwide to share data online. Like HTML (Hypertext Markup Language), XML is derived from SGML (Standard Generalized Markup Language). A *markup language* is a way to define a document's structure, identifying elements such as titles, headings, body text, tables, footnotes, and so on. HTML and SGML aren't practical for displaying highly structured documents on the Web—HTML can be too limited, and SGML is too complicated—so XML was designed to meet a growing need for a more flexible method.

HTML consists of defined tags, such as Title and Body. A *tag* is a command or identifier that specifies how a Web page is formatted or structured. For example, the Title tag in HTML is used to specify a Web page's title. With XML, you can define your own tags and use them to display data.

You can create XML documents in an application and then use the data in the XML file in any application. For example, XML files created in Access can be used in Word or Excel. In addition, different users can use different presentation formats to display the same data. The presentation format is specified in files called *Extensible Stylesheet Language* (XSL) files. XSL files specify how the data will be formatted when viewed on a Web page. You can store such information as the font color, size, and background color in the XSL file.

You can use XML and Access to exchange data between different file formats. Access 2003 can be used to import data from different formats into an XML format. For example, you can use Access to import a database created in Microsoft SQL Server into XML format. You can then export this XML data or display it on Web sites.

Exporting an Access object as an XML document

You use the Export XML dialog box, shown in Exhibit 4-1, to export an Access object as an XML document. By using this dialog box, you can export an object in the following ways:

- **Data (XML)** — To export both the object structure and the object data. This option creates a document with the extension .xml.
- **Schema of the data (XSD)** — To export only the object structure. This option creates a document with the extension .xsd (for XML Schema Definition).
- **Presentation of your data (XSL)** — To export the object data along with its formatting styles. This option creates two documents: one with the extension .htm, and one with the extension .xsl. This option is available only if the Data (XML) option is selected.

To export an Access object as an XML document:

1 Open the Export Table dialog box.
2 From the Save as type list, select XML Documents.
3 Click Export to open the Export XML dialog box.
4 In the dialog box, select the required options.
5 Click OK to export.
6 Close the database.

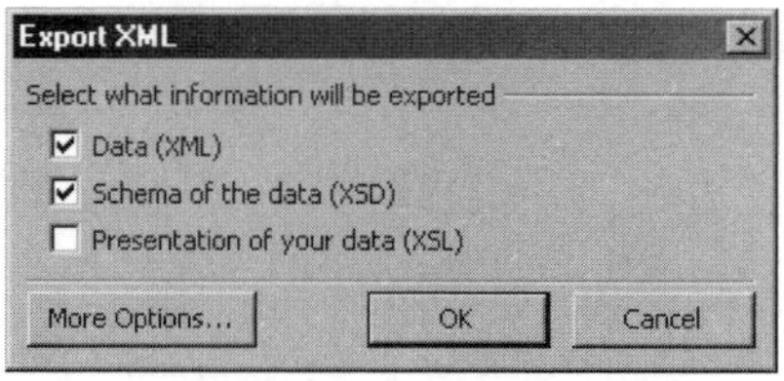

Exhibit 4-1: The Export XML dialog box

Importing an XML document

Use the Import XML dialog box to bring XML documents into an Access database. By using this dialog box, you can import both the structure and the data of the XML document. However, when you import an XML document, you must import the entire document, not just a portion of it.

To import an XML document into Access:

1 Open the required database.
2 Open the Import dialog box.
3 Select the XML or XSD document option.
4 Click Import.

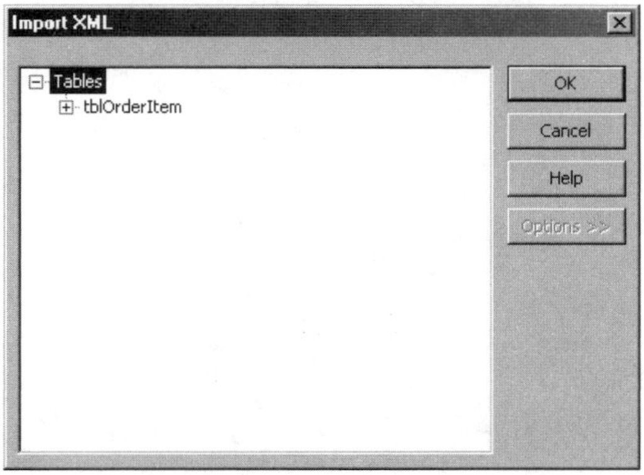

Exhibit 4-2: The Import XML dialog box

Do it!

A-1: Exporting and importing XML documents

Here's how	Here's why
1 Start Access	Click Start, and choose Programs, Microsoft Office, Microsoft Office Access 2003.
2 Open Objects	From the current unit folder. (If a security message is displayed, click Yes, and then click Open.)
3 Select **tblOrderItem**	(If necessary.) You'll export this table as an XML document.
4 Choose **File**, **Export...**	To open the Export Table 'tblOrderItem' To dialog box.
5 From the Save as type list, select **XML**	You'll export the table as an XML document.
In the File name box, verify that tblOrderItem appears	
6 Click **Export**	To open the Export XML dialog box. By default, the Data (XML) and Schema of the data (XSD) options are checked. You'll export both the schema and the data.
	A *schema* is a model that describes the information structure of an XML document. The schema document is called an XML Schema Definition (XSD).
7 Click **OK**	To export the table.
8 Close the database	
9 Open Import Objects	(If a security message is displayed, click Yes, and then click Open.) You'll import the XSD document, which stores the table structure, into this database.
Observe the tables of the Import Objects database	
10 Choose **File**, **Get External Data**, **Import...**	To open the Import dialog box.
From the Files of type list, select **XML**	To view the XML documents.
Select **tblOrderItem.xsd**	You'll import only the structure of the tblOrderItem table.
Click **Import**	To open the Import XML dialog box, as shown in Exhibit 4-2.

11	Click **OK**	A message box appears, indicating that the document has been imported.
	Click **OK**	The tblOrderItem1 table appears in the Database window.
12	Open tblOrderItem1	Only the table structure appears in the imported table.
	Close the table	
13	Delete **tblOrderItem1**	(Select the tblOrderItem1 table, and press Delete.) A message box appears, which prompts you to confirm the decision to delete this table.
	Click **Yes**	
14	Open the Import dialog box	(Choose File, Get External Data, Import.) You'll now import the XML document, which stores both the structure and data.
15	Select **tblOrderItem**	(If necessary.) This is the XML document.
	Click **Import**	To open the Import XML dialog box.
16	Click **OK**	A message box appears, indicating that the document has been imported.
	Click **OK**	The tblOrderItem1 table now appears in the Database window.
17	Open tblOrderItem1	Both the table structure and data have been imported.
	Close the table	
	Close the database	

Exporting an object with an XSL file

Explanation   You can display data in the same format as in the original document by exporting the database object along with an XSL file. When you export the database object with an XSL file, the presentation format is also exported. For example, if you export a table with its XSL file, the formatting of the table is also exported.

When you export a database object with its presentation format, Access automatically creates an XSL file and an HTML file for the database object. The XSL file describes how the data from the XML document will be displayed in the HTML document.

To export an Access object as an XML document with its XSL file:

1 Open the Export Table dialog box.
2 From the Save as type list, select XML Documents.
3 Click Export to open the Export XML dialog box.
4 In the Export XML dialog box, select all three options.
5 Click OK.

Do it!   ## A-2:   Exporting a database object as an XML document with its XSL file

Here's how	Here's why
1 Open Objects	If a security message is displayed, click Yes, and click Open.
2 Select **tblOrder**	You'll export this table as an XML document with its XSL file.
3 Choose **File**, **Export...**	To open the Export Table 'tblOrder' To dialog box.
From the Save as type list, select **XML**	
In the File name box, verify that tblOrder appears	
4 Click **Export**	To open the Export XML dialog box. By default, the Data (XML) and Schema of the data (XSD) options are checked.
5 Check **Presentation of your data (XSL)**	You'll export the document with its XSL file.
6 Click **OK**	To close the Export XML dialog box and to export the table.

7	Click **Start**	To open the Windows Start menu.
	Choose **Programs**, **Accessories**, **Windows Explorer**	To open the Windows Explorer window.
	Navigate to the current unit folder	In addition to tblOrder.xml and tblOrder.xsd, there are two more files related to the tblOrder table: tblOrder.htm and tblOrder.xsl. These two files were created because you checked the Presentation of your data (XSL) option.
8	Double-click **tblOrder.xml**	
		The file opens in Internet Explorer. This file displays only raw data.
	Close the browser	
9	Double-click **tblOrder.htm**	
		To open the document in Internet Explorer. The document displays both the table and data. The document displays data with its original formatting because you exported the table with its XSL file. The XSL file contains data-formatting information.
	Close the browser	
10	Double-click **tblOrder.xsl**	![tblOrder.xsl]
		To open the file in your browser. You can see the XSL file for the table in the HTML form. The XSL file describes how the data from the XML document is displayed in the HTML document.
	Close the browser	
	Close the Windows Explorer window	
	Close the database	
11	Close Access	

Topic B: XML and Excel 2003

Explanation

You can also export data from a workbook to an XML file. To export XML data, you must map the workbook to a user-defined XML schema (.xsd file) by using the XML Source task pane. By mapping, you're associating the workbook elements with an XML schema, thereby defining them for use in other applications.

The XML Source task pane

You can view and manipulate the fields in an Excel workbook by mapping it to an XML schema. You can do so by using the XML Source task pane. The task pane also provides options to import and export XML data. You can also refresh the imported data to reflect the latest changes in the source.

To map a workbook to an XML schema:

1 Choose Data, XML, XML Source to display the XML Source task pane.

2 In the task pane, click WorkBook Maps to open the XML Maps dialog box.

3 Click Add to open the Select XML Source dialog box. Browse to and locate the appropriate .xsd file, and click Open.

4 The Multiple Roots dialog box opens. Select the .xsd file, and click OK.

5 Click OK to close the XML Maps dialog box. The file and its elements appear in the XML Source task pane.

6 Drag the elements from the task pane to the corresponding cells in the workbook. The mapped areas appear in blue with nonprintable borders.

Exhibit 4-3: The XML Source task pane

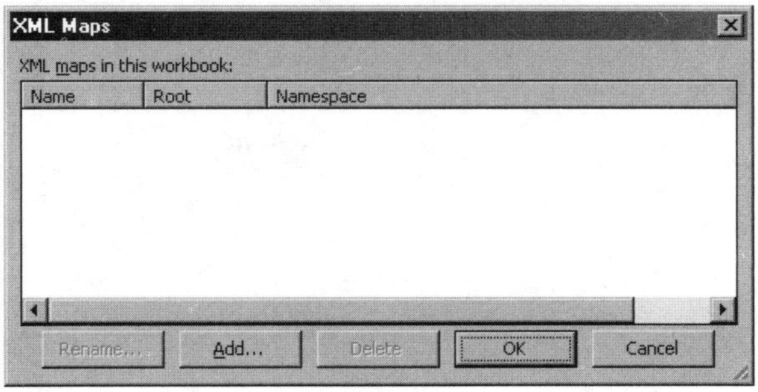

Exhibit 4-4: The XML Maps dialog box

Do it!

B-1: Using the XML Source task pane

Here's how	Here's why
1 Start Excel	Click Start, and choose Programs, Microsoft Office, Microsoft Office Excel 2003.
2 Open Employees	(From the current unit folder.) You'll create an XML map for this workbook.
3 Save the workbook as **My employees**	In the current unit folder.
4 Choose **Data**, **XML**, **XML Source...**	To display the XML Source task pane, shown in Exhibit 4-3.
5 Click **XML Maps**	(In the XML Source task pane.) To open the XML Maps dialog box, as shown in Exhibit 4-4.
Click **Add**	To open the Select XML Source dialog box.
In the Select XML Source dialog box, use the Look in list to navigate to the current unit folder	If necessary.
Select **EmployeeRecord**	This file contains the XML schema.
Click **Open**	
	The Multiple Roots dialog box opens, with EmployeeRecord selected.
Click **OK**	To close the Multiple Roots dialog box and return to the XML Maps dialog box. (If a message box appears, indicating that some schema elements and structures cannot be mapped to the worksheet, click Yes to continue.)

6   Click **OK**

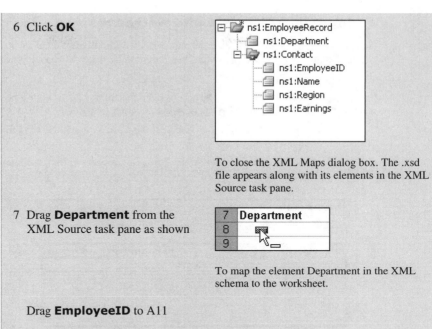

To close the XML Maps dialog box. The .xsd file appears along with its elements in the XML Source task pane.

7   Drag **Department** from the XML Source task pane as shown

7	Department
8	
9	

To map the element Department in the XML schema to the worksheet.

Drag **EmployeeID** to A11

Drag **Name** to B11

Drag **Region** to C11

Drag **Earnings** to D11

Importing XML data into workbooks

Explanation You can import data in XML format into a workbook after creating an XML map. You can then store this imported data in a database by using Microsoft Access.

To import XML data:

1 Choose Data, XML, Import to open the Import XML dialog box. You can also use the Import XML Data button on the List toolbar.

2 Select the XML file that contains the data. You can use the Look in list to locate the file, if necessary.

3 Click Import. The data in the XML file appears in the corresponding cells in the workbook.

Department				
Human resources				
EmployeeID ▾	Name ▾	Region ▾	Earnings ▾	
E001	Malcolm Pingault	East ◈	$73,500	
E006	Annie Philips	West	$60,000	
E011	Paul Anderson	East	$180,000	
E019	Jamie Morrison	East	$62,000	
✴				

Exhibit 4-5: The worksheet

Do it! ## B-2: Importing XML data into a workbook

Here's how	Here's why
1 Choose **Data**, **XML**, **Import...**	To open the Import XML dialog box.
2 Select **EmployeeInfo**	(From the current unit folder.) This file contains values for workbook fields, such as Department, EmployeeID, Name, Region, and Earnings.
3 Click **Import**	You'll see that the data corresponding to the Department, EmployeeID, Name, Region, and Earnings fields appear in the appropriate cells, as shown in Exhibit 4-5.
4 Update and close the workbook	

Exporting data from workbooks to XML data files

Explanation

You can export workbook data in XML format. This exported data can then be used by other applications, such as Access or Word. You can also add or delete records in the workbook. For data to be exported as XML, the workbook should contain a valid XML map.

To export the workbook data, you can choose Data, XML, Export, or use the Export XML Data button on the List toolbar.

```
<?xml version="1.0" encoding="UTF-8" standalone="yes" ?>
- <ns1:EmployeeRecord
    xmlns:ns1="http://MyEmployeeData/EmployeeRecord.xsd">
    <ns1:Department>Accounts</ns1:Department>
  - <ns1:Details>
      <ns1:EmployeeID>E002</ns1:EmployeeID>
      <ns1:Name>Shannon Lee</ns1:Name>
      <ns1:Region>South</ns1:Region>
      <ns1:Earnings>$80000</ns1:Earnings>
    </ns1:Details>
  - <ns1:Details>
      <ns1:EmployeeID>E007</ns1:EmployeeID>
      <ns1:Name>Melissa James</ns1:Name>
      <ns1:Region>East</ns1:Region>
      <ns1:Earnings>$87000</ns1:Earnings>
    </ns1:Details>
  - <ns1:Details>
      <ns1:EmployeeID>E015</ns1:EmployeeID>
      <ns1:Name>Sandra Lawrence</ns1:Name>
      <ns1:Region>North</ns1:Region>
      <ns1:Earnings>$100000</ns1:Earnings>
    </ns1:Details>
  - <ns1:Details>
      <ns1:EmployeeID>E017</ns1:EmployeeID>
      <ns1:Name>Kevin Meyers</ns1:Name>
```

Exhibit 4-6: The document My export as XML in Internet Explorer

Do it!

B-3: Exporting data from a workbook to an XML file

Here's how	Here's why
1 Open Export as XML	From the current unit folder.
2 Display the XML Source task pane	(If necessary, choose Data, XML, XML Source.) You'll see that the workbook is mapped to EmployeeRecord.
3 Save the workbook as **My export as XML**	
4 In A21, type **E039**	To enter the Employee ID for a new record.
In B21, enter **Raoul Duke**	
In C21, enter **North**	
Copy the data from D17 cell to D21	An error appears because there is a number stored as text.
Select A16:D16	To select the record for Anna Morris.
Choose **Edit**, **Delete Row**	To delete the record.
5 Update the workbook	
6 Choose **Data**, **XML**, **Export...**	To open the Export XML dialog box.
From the Save in list, select the current unit folder	If necessary.
In the File name box, enter **My export as XML**	
7 Click **Export**	To export the workbook as an XML file.
8 Close the workbook	
9 Close Excel	
10 Open the My export as XML document in the Internet Explorer	(From the current unit folder.) The document My export as XML appears, as shown in Exhibit 4-6.
11 Close the Internet Explorer	

Topic C: XML and Word 2003

Explanation

You can use Word 2003 to create and edit XML documents. You can also import an XML document and attach an XML schema.

Creating XML documents

In Word 2003, you can create XML documents by saving Word documents in XML format. For example, you can save a Word document with employee information as an XML document. You can then use this XML document to display employee information on a Web site. You can also use this XML document in other office applications, such as Excel and Access.

To save data from a word document as an XML document:

1   Create a new document.
2   Enter the contents of the document.
3   Choose File, Save As to open the Save As dialog box.
4   From the Files of type list, select XML Document.
5   Specify a name for the document.
6   Click Save.

Do it!   **C-1:   Creating an XML document**

Here's how	Here's why
1 Start Word	
2 Create a blank document	Open the New Document task pane, and click Blank document.
3 Type as shown	100 Ann Salinski 224 Maple Street Mill Valley CA 90952
	To enter employee information for Ann Salinski.
4 Click **File**, **Save**	The Save As dialog box opens.
In the File name box, type **AnnSalinski details**	
From the Save as type list box, select **XML Document**	You can now use this XML document with other office applications. You can also use the XML document to display employee information on a Web site.
Click **Save**	To save the document and close the Save As dialog box.
5 Close the document	

Inserting an XML file into a Word document

Explanation

You can insert XML data into a Word document. For example, you can insert employee data stored in an XML file into a Word document, and then use Word to edit the information. You can then save the document in Word format or XML format.

To insert an XML file into a Word document:

1 Open a Word document.
2 Choose Insert, Insert File to open the Insert File dialog box.
3 From the Files of type list, select XML Files.
4 Select the XML file that you want to insert. You can use the Look in list to locate the file.
5 Click Insert.
6 Choose File, Save As to save the document as a Word document.

Do it!

C-2: Inserting an XML document

Here's how	Here's why
1 Create a blank document	
2 Choose **Insert**, **File...**	To open the Insert File dialog box. You'll insert an XML file into this document.
From the Files of type list, select **XML Files**	
Navigate to the current unit folder	If necessary.
Select **EmpDet**	
3 Click **Insert**	To insert the contents of the XML file into the document.
4 Choose **File**, **Save As...**	To open the Save As dialog box.
Navigate to the current unit folder	If necessary.
From the Save as type list, select **Word Document**	If necessary.
Edit the File name box to read **JohnWilkins details**	To name the file.
5 Click **Save**	
6 Close the document	

Attaching an XML schema

Explanation
When you create your own tags in XML, you need to specify a schema to identify the tags. A *schema* is a model that describes the information structure of the XML document. The schema used with an XML document is known as an *XML Schema Definition* (XSD). An XSD is used to describe and validate data in an XML document. Before you create an XML document, you need to define an XSD. Exhibit 4-7 shows a sample XSD:

```
<xsd:schema xmlns:xsd="http://www.w3.org/2001/XMLSchema">

        <xsd:annotation>
         <xsd:documentation xml:lang="en">
           Employee Details schema for Outlander Spices.com
         </xsd:documentation>
        </xsd:annotation>

        <xsd:element name="empDetails" type="Empdetails"/>
        <xsd:complexType name="Empdetails">
         <xsd:sequence>
                <xsd:element name="Empno" type="xsd:int"/>
                <xsd:element name="FirstName" type="xsd:string"/>
                <xsd:element name="LastName" type="xsd:string"/>
                <xsd:element name="Address" type="USAddress"/>
         </xsd:sequence>
        </xsd:complexType>

        <xsd:complexType name="USAddress">
         <xsd:sequence>
                <xsd:element name="Street" type="xsd:string"/>
                <xsd:element name="City" type="xsd:string"/>
                <xsd:element name="State" type="xsd:string"/>
                <xsd:element name="Zip" type="xsd:decimal"/>
         </xsd:sequence>
        </xsd:complexType>
</xsd:schema>
```

Exhibit 4-7: A sample XSD

After you create an XSD, you can create an XML document based on the schema, as shown in Exhibit 4-8.

```
<?xml version="1.0" ?>
- <empDetails>
    <Empno>100</Empno>
    <FirstName>John</FirstName>
    <LastName>Wilkins</LastName>
  - <Address>
      <Street>223 Maple Street</Street>
      <City>Mill Valey</City>
      <State>CA</State>
      <Zip>90952</Zip>
    </Address>
  </empDetails>
```

Exhibit 4-8: Sample XML code

You can also use Word to create an XML document based on a schema. To do this, you must attach a schema to the Word document. To do so:

1　Create a new document.

2　Open the XML Structure task pane.

3　Click Template and Add-Ins to open the Templates and Add-ins dialog box.

4　Click Add Schema to open the Add Schema dialog box.

5　Select the schema.

6　Click Open.

7　Specify a name for the schema.

8　Click OK.

9　Click OK.

After attaching the schema to a Word document, you can apply tags to document content and then save the document as an XML document. To apply a tag to specific text, you select the text and then select the relevant tag from the "Choose an element to apply to your current selection" list. This list is in the XML Structure task pane. After tags are applied, the XML document can be used to add information to a database because the data is now arranged in a specific structure.

You can also delete a schema attached to a Word document. To do this:

1　Open an XML document.

2　Open the Templates and Add-ins dialog box.

3　Click Schema Library to open the Schema Library dialog box.

4　Select the schema.

5　Click Delete Schema.

6　Click OK.

7　Click OK.

Do it!

C-3:　Attaching an XML schema to a Word document

Here's how	Here's why
1　Create a blank document	Open the New Document task pane, and click Blank document.
Type as shown	1001 Western Spice Retailers 140 Summit Ave San Francisco CA 94138
2　Choose **View**, **Task Pane**	(If necessary.) To open the Getting Started task pane.
From the Other Task Panes list, select **XML Structure**	To open the XML Structure task pane.

3 Click **Templates and Add-Ins...**	To open the Templates and Add-ins dialog box. The XML Schema tab is activated.
Click **Add Schema**	To open the Add Schema dialog box. You'll attach an XML schema to this document.
Navigate to the current unit folder	
Select **Cust**	
Click **Open**	The Schema Settings dialog box opens.
4 In the URI box, type **Customer schema**	To name the schema.
Click **OK**	To close the Schema Settings dialog box.
5 Click **OK**	To close the Templates and Add-ins dialog box and to attach the schema to the document.
6 Select the entire document	Press Ctrl+A.
From the Choose an element to apply to your current selection list, select **Customer {Customer schema}**	(In the XML Structure task pane.) The Apply to entire document? dialog box opens.
Click **Apply to Entire Document**	To apply the first element in the XML schema to the entire document. The Customer tag is applied to the entire document.
Press (END)	To deselect the text.
7 Select as shown	You'll apply a tag to this selection.
From the Choose an element to apply to your current selection list, select **Idno**	(In the XML Structure task pane.) To apply the Idno tag to 1001.
Apply the **CustomerName** tag to **Western Spice Retailers**	Select "Western Spice Retailers," and from the Choose an element to apply to your current selection list, select CustomerName.

8 Select as shown

From the Choose an element to apply to your current selection list, select **Address**

To apply the Address tag to the entire selection.

9 Press `END`

To deselect the text.

10 Select as shown

You'll regroup the text under the Address tag.

11 From the Choose an element to apply to your current selection list, select **Street**

To apply the Street tag to the selection.

Apply the **City** tag to **San Francisco**

Apply the **State** tag to **CA**

Apply the **Zip** tag to **94138**

The text is now regrouped under the respective tags.

12 Choose **File**, **Save As...**

To open the Save As dialog box.

Edit the File name box to read **Prospective customer**

From the Save as type list, select **XML Document**

13 Click **Save**

To save the document as an XML document.

14 Close the document

15 Close Word

Unit summary: XML and Office 2003

Topic A   In this topic, you learned how to **export and import XML documents** in Access. You also learned how to **export a database object** to an XML document with its XSL file.

Topic B   In this topic, you learned how to use the **XML Source task pane** in Excel. You learned how to **import XML data** into a workbook. You also learned how to **export data** from a workbook to an XML data file.

Topic C   In this topic, you learned how to **create an XML document** and how to **insert an XML file** in Word. You also learned how to **attach an XML schema** to a Word document by using the **XML Structure task pane**.

Independent practice activity

1 Start Access.

2 Open Practice Objects.

3 Export the tblEmployee table from Practice Objects as an XML document with its XSL file.

4 Close the database.

5 Close Access.

6 Start Excel.

7 Open Exporting practice.

8 Save the workbook as **My exporting practice**.

9 Activate the XML worksheet. Create a workbook map by using EmployeeRecord.xsd, and link the elements in the file to the corresponding fields in the workbook. (*Hint:* In the XML Source task pane, click XML Maps.)

10 Close the XML Source task pane and the List toolbar.

11 Close My exporting practice. (*Hint:* Do not save the changes.)

12 Close Excel.

13 Start Word.

14 Open a blank document, and type **This file provides the details of the customer**.

15 Save the document, in Word Document format, as **My customer**.

16 Insert the file ImportantCust into the document. (*Hint:* Select All Files from the Files of type list.)

17 Save the document as an XML document named **Customer details**, and close it.

18 Create a new document with the information shown in Exhibit 4-9.

19 Attach the schema Emp.xsd to this document, and specify the URI name as **Employee schema**.

20 Apply the empDetails, Empno, FirstName, LastName, Address, Street, City, State, and Zip tags, as shown in Exhibit 4-10.

21 Save the document as an XML document named **Manager details**.

22 Close the document, and close Word.

```
105
Carol Jones
817 Ester Ave
Portland
OR
97209
```

Exhibit 4-9: The data for Step 6 of the Independent Practice Activity

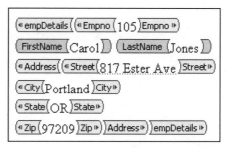

Exhibit 4-10: The tags to be attached for Step 8 of the Independent Practice Activity

Appendix A

Using Windows SharePoint Services

This appendix covers this additional topic:

A Getting started with SharePoint.

Topic A: Getting started with SharePoint

Explanation

It's becoming easier to share documents with co-workers and to integrate Office applications. With Microsoft SharePoint Services, you can create a *Shared Workspace*, a Microsoft Windows SharePoint Services site where team members can share documents and exchange information. By using SharePoint Services and Office 2003, team members can build and manage content and create new Web sites for projects and meetings. SharePoint Services can also facilitate communication. You can find a team member online, or add comments and results to a Shared Workspace.

You can open the SharePoint Services site in a Web browser or use the Shared Workspace task pane in Word 2003, Excel 2003, or PowerPoint 2003. The Microsoft Windows SharePoint site can be a regular site, a Meeting Workspace site, or a Document Workspace site. A *Meeting Workspace* is designed to share information and materials, such as agenda documents, decisions, and meeting attendees. A *Document Workspace* is designed to share documents among members of a project team.

The Shared Workspace task pane

The Shared Workspace task pane displays information about a Document Workspace, such as the workspace participants, the list of tasks, and the hyperlinks shared among the team members. You can use the Shared Workspace task pane in all of the Office 2003 applications. To display this task pane in PowerPoint, open a PowerPoint presentation and then choose Tools, Shared Workspace (shown in Exhibit 1-1).

When you open a document—such as a Word document, an Excel worksheet, or a PowerPoint presentation—that is in a Document Workspace, the Shared Workspace task pane automatically opens in the application. For example, when you open a PowerPoint presentation in a Document Workspace, the presentation opens with the Shared Workspace task pane.

You can view the members of the Document Workspace and their online status by selecting the Members tab. You can also add new team members to the Document Workspace and define their roles if you have administrative powers. The roles that you can assign to your team members include:

- **Reader** — Has permission to read the documents in the Document Workspace.
- **Contributor** — Has permission to add content to the documents in the Document Workspace.
- **Web Designer** — Has permission to create lists and document libraries and to customize pages in a Web site.
- **Administrator** — Has full control over the Document Workspace.

Exhibit 1-1: A sample Shared Workspace task pane

The following table lists the various tabs available in the Shared Workspace task pane:

Tab	Description
Status	Displays the restrictions or errors in a document in the Document Workspace.
Members	Displays the names and online status of team members who have the rights to access the site.
Tasks	Displays the tasks assigned to different members of the team.
Documents	Displays the documents in a Document Workspace.
Links	Displays the links available in a Document Workspace.
Document Information	Displays documentation information, such as the creator of the document and the date when the document was last modified.

Do it!

A-1: Exploring the Shared Workspace task pane

Questions and answers

1 What is a Shared Workspace?

2 You can open a SharePoint site by using a Web browser. True or false?

3 Which tab in the Shared Workspace task pane is used to list the documents in the Document Workspace?

4 In the Shared Workspace task pane, you can view the online status of the members of a Document Workspace. True or false?

5 Using the Shared Workspace task pane, you can add new documents to your Document Workspace. True or false?

About sharing documents

Explanation

You can use the Shared Workspace task pane to share documents or to open Document Workspaces. The following table describes the features of a SharePoint Services site:

Features	Description
Document library	You can store documents that all members of the Shared Workspace can use.
Task list	You can assign tasks with due dates to members.
Link list	You can add a hyperlink so that members can access the required information.
Member list	You can see the user names of the members.
E-mail alerts	You can receive notifications regarding the changes made in a document in the Shared Workspace.

About adding users

You can create a Document Workspace and then add users to it. To create a Document Workspace, you should have the permission to do this at the Microsoft Windows SharePoint Services site.

In PowerPoint 2003, you can create a Document Workspace by using the Shared Workspace task pane. To do so:

1 Open a presentation in Microsoft PowerPoint 2003.
2 Choose Tools, Shared Workspace to open the Shared Workspace task pane.
3 In the Location for new workspace box, type the Web address of the SharePoint server.
4 In the Shared Workspace task pane, click the Create button to create the Document Workspace.

After creating the Document Workspace, you can add users to it. To do so:

1 Open Microsoft Outlook 2003.
2 Choose File, New, Mail Message to open a new message.
3 In the To and Cc boxes, enter the e-mail addresses of the people you would like to include as members of the Document Workspace.
4 In the Subject box, type the subject of the message.
5 Choose Insert, File to open Insert File dialog box.
6 Select the file you want to add to the Document Workspace, and click Insert.
7 In the Attachment Options task pane, under Send attachments as, select Shared attachments.
8 In the Create Document Workspace at box, type the Web address of the Microsoft Windows SharePoint site.
9 Type the message in the message area, and click Send.

Meeting Workspaces

You can use a Meeting Workspace to plan, conduct, and review the outcomes of meetings. For example, you can add documents and tasks related to a meeting or obtain information about a meeting. A Meeting Workspace is made up of one or more pages containing information such as meeting objectives and agenda, the list of attendees, the decisions made, and the follow-up items generated during the meeting.

Creating a Meeting Workspace

Using Outlook 2003, you can set up a Meeting Workspace site by first creating a New Meeting Request and then clicking the Meeting Services button. A Meeting Request is a message sent to invite people to a meeting.

To create a new Meeting Workspace for an existing meeting request:

1   Open Outlook 2003.
2   Choose File, New, Meeting Request to open the Meeting window.
3   Click Meeting Workspace to display the Meeting Workspace task pane.
4   In the Meeting Workspace task pane, click Change settings.
5   In the Meeting Workspace task pane, under Select a location, from the list, select a location for your workspace.
6   Select Create a new workspace, if necessary.
7   Select a template language and template type.
8   Click OK.
9   Click Create.

You can remove a Meeting Workspace link from a meeting request by clicking Remove in the Meeting Workspace task pane.

Do it!

A-2:   Discussing the Meeting Workspace

Questions and answers
1 For what purpose do you use a Meeting Workspace?
2 You can create a Meeting Workspace with the help of Outlook 2003. True or false?
3 You can remove a Meeting Workspace link from a meeting request by clicking Delete in the Meeting Workspace task pane. True or false?

Appendix B

Infopath and OneNote

This appendix covers these additional topics:

A Infopath.

B OneNote.

Topic A: Infopath

Explanation

You can use Infopath to create forms that can be used to gather, share, reuse, and manage information. A *form* is a document with a set of controls through which users can enter information. You can store this information in a database, on a Web server, in a file share, or on a server running Windows SharePoint Services. For example, a marketing manager might design an Infopath form so that staff members can enter information about competitive products. After the forms are filled out, the marketing manager might summarize the names of the firm's largest competitors, their product offerings, and their prices.

Designing forms

Infopath is designed for two distinct tasks: designing forms and filling out forms. You can also merge forms and share your forms with other users.

To design a form:

1 Click Start, and choose Programs, Microsoft Office, Microsoft Office InfoPath 2003 to start InfoPath, as shown in Exhibit B-1.
2 Create a form layout.
3 Add controls to the form.
4 Bind controls to the data source.
5 Create views.
6 Publish the form.

Exhibit B-1: The Microsoft Office InfoPath 2003 application

Creating a form layout

You can create a form layout by using layout tables. A *layout table* is a collection of cells used to arrange and organize form contents. Layout tables help you define the dimensions and order of the areas in which you'll place text, images, and contents. To insert a table layout, drag a layout table from the Layout task pane into the desired location on your form.

To create a form layout, choose File, Design a Form to switch to design mode. The Design a Form task pane appears, as shown in Exhibit B-2. Then, click New Blank Form to create a new form.

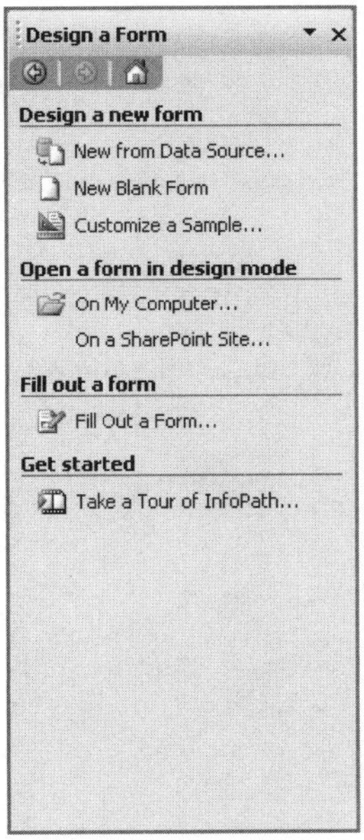

Exhibit B-2: The Design a Form task pane

Adding controls to the form

After you have created the form layout, you can add functionality by inserting controls. A *control* is a graphical user object—such as a text box, check box, or command button—that controls your program. The following table describes the various types of controls:

Controls	Description
Standard controls	Used to enter commonly used controls, such as text boxes and check boxes.
Repeating and optional controls	Used to insert list items, rows, or optional information.
Hyperlink and picture controls	Used to link addresses depending on the data, and used to insert pictures.
Buttons and expression boxes	Used to perform actions. Expression boxes are read-only text controls.

To insert a control:

1 Place the insertion point where you want to insert the control.
2 In the Design Tasks task pane, click Controls to display the Controls task pane, as shown in Exhibit B-3.
3 Check the Automatically create data source check box, if necessary.
4 Click the control you want to insert.

Exhibit B-3: The Controls task pane

Binding controls to the data source

After you insert controls in a form, you must bind them to the data source. *Binding* is the process of connecting a control to a field to ensure that data entered in the control is saved. A *field* is an element in the data source that saves the information that is inserted into the control. While a control enables you to insert data, the associated field determines the data type that can be used. For example, the date picker control enables you to enter a date, and its field saves only those values that are dates.

To add a field:

1　Choose View, Data source. The Data Source task pane appears.

2　In the task pane, right-click the required field. A menu appears.

3　Choose Add. The Add Field or Group dialog box appears, as shown in Exhibit B-4.

4　In the Name box, type the name of the new field.

5　From the Type list, select an element field.

6　From the Data Type list, select the data type of the field.

7　Click OK to close the dialog box and to apply the changes.

When you design forms, you can either have fields created automatically when a control is inserted or bind controls to existing fields by using the "Automatically create the data source" check box in the Controls task pane.

Exhibit B-4: The Add Field or Group dialog box

Creating views

The form you create has a default view, called View 1. To select a default view:

1 Choose View, Manage Views. The Views task pane appears, as shown in Exhibit B-5.

2 Click the drop-down arrow next to the view that you want to designate as the default view.

3 Choose Set as Default.

You can modify the default view and create a custom view. You can also set background color, borders and shading, layout width, and text-formatting options for the default view. When designing a form, you can switch between views by selecting a view from the Select a view list in the Views task pane.

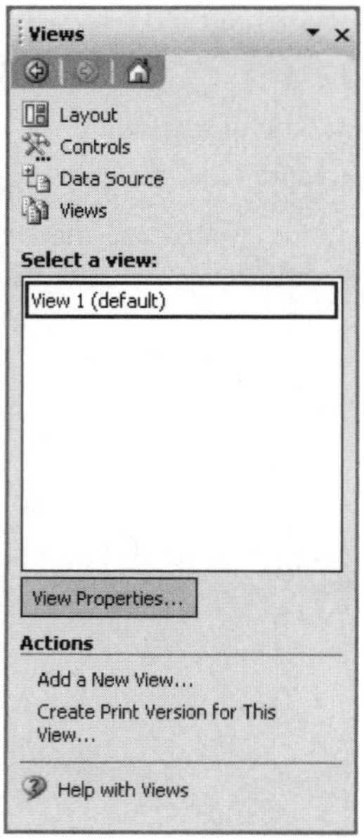

Exhibit B-5: The Views task pane

Publishing the form

You can publish a form to a shared location to make it available to other users. Before publishing your form, you need to save it and test it by previewing. When you save a form in design mode, you are actually saving a form template. A *form template* is a file or set of files that determines the data structure, appearance, and behavior of the form.

To publish a form:

1 Choose File, Save As to open the Microsoft InfoPath dialog box.
2 Click Publish to open the Publishing Wizard, shown in Exhibit B-6.
3 Click Next to move to the next step of the wizard.
4 Verify that "To a shared folder on this computer or on a network" is selected, and then click Next.
5 Type the path and the file name where you want to publish the form. Type a name for the form in the Form name box, and click Next.
6 Verify that the location is correct, and click Finish.
7 Check "Open this form from its published location," and click Close. The form you created opens as Form1.
8 Close the Form.

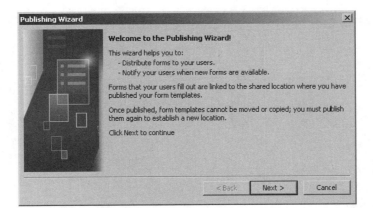

Exhibit B-6: The Publishing Wizard

Using forms

After you design a form, you can fill it out. To fill out a form:

1 Choose File, Fill Out a Form. The Fill Out a Form task pane appears, as shown in Exhibit B-7.

2 Click the form name. The form opens.

3 Enter the data.

Infopath checks the data you enter in a form and displays an error message if the data does not match the data validation condition specified in design mode. The data validation condition refers to conditions such as a range of permissible values or the data type that you can enter into a control.

Exhibit B-7: The Fill Out a Form task pane

Sharing and merging forms

You can share your forms with other users by sending forms as e-mail messages, by exporting forms to the Web, or by submitting form data to a database.

You can merge multiple forms created from the same template. To do so:

1 Open the template.

2 Choose File, Merge forms. The Merge Forms dialog box opens.

3 Specify the files you want to merge with the form.

4 Click Merge.

Topic B: OneNote

Explanation

You can use OneNote to take notes in a meeting or a lecture and then organize, share, or reuse your notes on a laptop, desktop, or Tablet PC. OneNote is available as a stand-alone program only. It is not included in any of the Office 2003 editions. Click Start, and choose Programs, Microsoft Office, Microsoft Office OneNote2003 to start OneNote, as shown in Exhibit B-8.

Exhibit B-8: The Microsoft Office OneNote 2003 application

Understanding the user interface

OneNote is a stand-alone program, but it also integrates with other Microsoft Office System Programs. The following table describes the five important elements in the user interface of OneNote:

Elements	Description
Page	Contains a surface for taking notes.
Page header	Contains a title area and the automatic date and time stamp. The Page header is located at the top of the page.
Section tabs	Contain information on the different sections of your notes. The Section tabs enable you to access the sections.
Page tabs	Contain information on individual pages within each section. The Page tab shows the number of the page.
Menus and toolbars	Contain commands and buttons to perform different actions.

Taking notes

You can take notes on pages. To create a page, choose Insert, New Page, and type a title for the page in the Title box. After you create a page, you can write or type your notes on it. To type notes, click where you want to type the notes, and then type. To write notes by using a pen-input device, click the Pen button on the Standard toolbar, and then write your notes.

You can add graphics or text from a Web page and then rearrange the items by dragging them on your note page. OneNote saves your notes automatically when you're working or when you close a section.

Organizing notes

You can organize your notes into sections. To create a section, choose Insert, New Section. Type a title for the new area. After you create a section, you can move the required pages to it. To move a page to a section:

1 Right-click the page tab. A menu appears.
2 Choose Move Page To, Another Section to open the Move or Copy Pages dialog box, shown in Exhibit B-9.
3 Select Another Section.
4 Click Move.

You can also add note flags to your notes to access them easily. A *note flag* is a symbol that provides additional information about a note.

Exhibit B-9: The Move or Copy Pages dialog box

Sharing notes

You can share your notes with other users by sending the notes through e-mail or storing them at a shared location. To send notes in e-mail:

1 Select the page tabs of the pages you want to send.
2 Click E-mail on the Standard toolbar.
3 Type the recipient's e-mail address in the To box.
4 Click Send a Copy.

Office 2003:
New Features

Course summary

This summary contains information to help you bring the course to a successful conclusion. Using this information, you will be able to:

A Use the summary text to reinforce what you've learned in class.

B Determine other resources that might help you continue to learn about Microsoft Office 2003.

Topic A: Course summary

Use the following summary text to reinforce what you've learned in class.

Office 2003: New Features

Unit 1

In this unit, you learned how to use **Assistance** to find additional help from the Microsoft Office Online site. You learned how to download **additional templates** for Office 2003 applications by using the Microsoft Office Online Template site. You also learned how to download **additional clip art** by using the **Clip art on Office Online** option. You learned how to use **fax services** to send faxes. You learned how to access **Web-based online services** and how to **download third-party software** from the Microsoft Office Online Office Marketplace Web page. You also learned how to search for updates by using the **Check for Updates** option. You learned about **Instant Messaging**. You also learned how to use the **Research task pane**.

Unit 2

In this unit, you learned about the **accessibility** features in Word 2003. You also learned how to **switch** to **Reading Layout view** by using the **Read button** on the Standard toolbar. In addition, you learned how to **insert voice comments** by using the **Reviewing toolbar**. You also learned how to **restrict formatting styles** and **protect documents** by using the **Protect Document task pane**. Next, you learned how to **apply smart tags** to cells in Excel 2003 and how to use **smart tags** in PowerPoint 2003. You also learned how to use the **Thesaurus** in PowerPoint and how to **package a presentation** for use on a CD.

Unit 3

In this unit, you learned about the **Smart Tags property** in Access. You also learned about the **property propagation** feature. In addition, you learned about **database object dependencies** and how to **back up a database**. You learned how to **check for errors in forms**. You also learned how to use **search folders** in Outlook 2003. You learned how to **assign a flag to a message** and you **examined the Junk E-mail Filter**. You also learned how to **integrate the Calendar and contact information**.

Unit 4

In this unit, you learned how to **export and import XML documents** in Access. You also learned how to **export a database object** to an XML document with its XSL file. You also learned how to use the **XML Source task pane** in Excel. You learned how to **import XML data** in a workbook and how to **export data** from a workbook to an XML file. Then, you learned how to **create an XML document** in Word and how to insert an XML file into a Word document. You learned how to **attach an XML schema** to a Word document by using the **XML Structure task pane**.

Topic B: Continued learning after class

It is impossible to learn to use any software effectively in a single day. To get the most out of this class, you should begin working with Microsoft Office 2003 to perform real tasks as soon as possible. Course Technology also offers resources for continued learning.

Next courses in this series

This is the only course in this series.

Other resources

For more information, visit www.course.com.

Office 2003: New Features

Quick reference

Button	Function
→	Displays information based on keywords specified in the Search for box of a Web page
▣	Switches to Reading Layout view in Word
▨	Inserts a voice comment in Word
●	Starts recording the voice comment
■	Stops recording
⬒	Displays and closes the Reviewing pane
◈	Displays a menu that shows a set of options to correct or ignore an error

Index